Journeys
of Hope

Journeys
of Hope

30
TRUE STORIES
of Faith in Adversity

Collected by Allison Gappa Bottke
Founder of the God Allows U-Turns Project,
with Cheryll Hutchings

BARBOUR
PUBLISHING

The author is represented by Alive Communications, Inc., 7680 Goddard St., Suite 200, Colorado Springs, Colorado 80920.

Published by Barbour Publishing, Inc., P.O. Box 719, Uhrichsville, Ohio 44683
www.barbourbooks.com

Our mission is to publish and distribute inspirational products offering exceptional value and biblical encouragement to the masses.

 Member of the
Evangelical Christian
Publishers Association

Printed in the United States of America.
5 4 3 2 1

Contents

Introduction

A yellowed envelope. A twenty-four-hour dentist. A goldfish named Fluffy. A thirty-year-old Nativity set. Often we find hope in surprising, unusual places. It is God's way of reminding us that He is always with us, especially when we're sidetracked by the trials of life.

The thirty compelling stories in this book, the best of the God Allows U-Turns Project, offer us a glimpse of the extraordinary found in the everyday. They exemplify the love, peace, faith, and forgiveness found in times of desperation, moments of prayer, and exaltations of joy.

There is hope for the hopeless. There is relief from suffering. While you read, we invite you to lay down your concerns and experience a moment's rest from the "world weariness" that often marks our days and troubles our nights. With the richness of an unexpected surprise, these true stories of hope provide a vision into the life God wants us to experience with Him.

The Perspective of a Pansy
by Laura Smith, Roswell, Georgia

In Atlanta, we have the luxury of planting pansies in the fall and viewing their curious faces all winter long. That is how my grandma described their blossoms—as "faces." You know what? She was right. If you look into a pansy's velvet petals, you can see its eager expression peeking out at you. It was my grandmother's love for this flower that drew me to *Viola tricolor* hortensis when I was a little girl. My favorites were the white petals with purple centers, or "faces." They remain my favorite flower today.

Since pansies are annuals, last year's flowers had long since died and been pulled from the ground, never to be seen again. I hadn't taken the time to plant even one flat of pansy seedlings this fall. Actually, I hadn't found the time to do much of anything but work since September. My job had become especially demanding due to a project that required me to fly weekly to Washington, D.C.

Between airports, delayed flights, cancellations, taxicabs, trains, and countless hotel rooms, I hadn't spent enough time with my husband, hadn't returned phone calls from my parents, hadn't sent birthday cards to my dearest friends, and certainly hadn't made time to focus on God and His plans for my life. Most important, I hadn't taken the necessary time to come to terms with the death of my beloved grandma.

Perhaps by skipping the whole pansy planting process this autumn, I was putting off facing the reality that Grandma, the only grandparent I had ever known, had died. My connection between her and the flowers was so strong. I told myself I was just "too busy" for gardening enough times that I convinced myself it was true.

As I drove home from the airport one chilly November evening, I was overwhelmed by an empty pang in my heart. It had begun as a slight ache that Thursday and had built up to a deep hollow throb after five straight days of deadlines, lists, conference calls, and meetings.

I hadn't allowed any time for myself to read, visit with friends and family, or even pray. I had tried to ignore this vacuous feeling inside of me. I had just kept going and going, like a robot following programmed commands, forgetting about all of the things in life that gave it deeper meaning.

The pain was especially great this particular evening due to a canceled flight that delayed my getting home until long after my lonely husband was already in bed. After fighting eight lanes of stop-and-go traffic for over an hour, caused by what appeared to be a fatal accident, I arrived home frazzled. As I pulled into my driveway, my headlights shone into the empty flower beds. I glimpsed something white resting on the ground. I parked my car in the garage and walked around to the front yard to collect what

I assumed was a piece of garbage and throw it away. But I did not find any trash. Instead, I found a lone white pansy with a purple face flourishing in a barren bed of pine straw.

The determined flower had fought all odds to spring from a ripped-up root, which is not bred for regrowth, to return this year. It didn't seem possible, and maybe it wasn't. Yet here was a perfect posy grinning at me and asking me from its remarkable face why I, too, couldn't break through the soil and let myself bloom. If loved ones who have passed away can speak to us from heaven, I knew this was Grandma's way of letting me know that although she had left this earth, she wasn't really gone. Just like the pansy, which had been pulled from the dirt yet was still blossoming, my grandmother's spirit would always flourish inside my heart and with God.

Grandma never would have put work first. Her family and friends were the priorities in her world. She didn't know the meaning of timetables or of deadlines. Although her life was simple, she was always happy and saw only the good in others and the beauty in the world around her.

Hers was an example God would be proud of, one that I should follow. Perhaps it was time to open up my heart and my eyes to the important things around me, to fill up the empty hole inside me with the nourishment that only God could give me. Work could wait. Life, as the pansy showed me (through God's miraculous powers), could not.

A Hard Winter's Prayer
by Lynn Roaten Terrell, Wichita, Kansas

It was a hard winter—not just because it was especially cold, but because it was especially lean. The recession had permeated the country, and it was starting to affect entire communities.

We had suddenly been laid off from the aerospace industry, and there were no pantries of canned goods to see us through. Even the temporary construction jobs had dried up; so, until spring, there was no work at all. To complicate matters, our rental house was being sold, so we would have to move. And our baby needed medicine—expensive medicine. With no insurance, that was our major concern that cold Wednesday afternoon.

"If worse comes to worst, maybe we could manage an apartment building," I remarked, turning to the classifieds. "At least it would pay the rent, the utilities, and the phone. I'm sure Mr. Hill would extend our credit at his store through the winter," I encouraged my husband.

"But we can't buy the baby's medicine from the grocer," he observed.

Also, with thousands of people out of work—and with no apartment experience—we weren't even confident in our ability to land one of only three manager's positions listed in the paper.

I asked the Lord for guidance as I reached for the phone, then jumped in surprise at its sudden ring. The caller was a distant relative—very distant—someone new to the family whom we had met only twice. I barely knew her name.

"I hate to bother you," she apologized, "but we have a friend who has an apartment building, and his manager has to be in Florida in a week for a new job. He is desperate for a replacement, and I offered to ask around. Do you happen to know of anyone who might be interested?"

My heart raced as I finished my interrupted prayer with a silent but rousing *Thank You, Lord!* But aloud I managed to maintain my composure. "Where is it?" I asked.

It was just a few miles from us. I had even lived there for a year when I was a teenager.

When we met with the owner that evening, he explained that he had another business across town, and he wanted us to move that weekend when he could help. The timing was perfect!

"That's fine," my husband said, "but we need to take care of something very important. Could you also hire me for some extra work so I could make some cash?"

"Sure. And if you need anything from my store, I can just deliver it on my way home. In fact, I'll just run a tab for you, and you can work it off by painting."

"Oh, thank you for the job, Mr. Hanson," we exclaimed in excitement. "But we've already arranged for groceries."

"Well, good; I don't own a grocery store." He laughed while chewing on his cigar stub. "And just call me Doc. I'm a pharmacist."

Even as God was arranging the job for the former manager, He had met our future needs.

Amen! I silently prayed, formally ending one more prayer that had been answered—even before we bowed our heads.

Are You Sitting Down?
by Sandy Sheppard, Vassar, Michigan

My heart thumped excitedly as I dialed my sister's number and waited for her to pick up her phone 2,500 miles away. *Life is so unpredictable,* I reflected. When my husband, Rick, and I married twenty-one-and-a-half years ago, we had things all planned out. I'd teach school while he attended seminary; then he would pastor a church and we'd have a baby.

Some of our plans worked out rather well. I taught for five years; Rick graduated and became associate pastor of a large city church. Everything except the matter of having a baby.

I waited for my sister's phone to ring and thought of other calls and other times. The phone, an impersonal bearer of personal information, had played a large role in my life. Some calls had brought tears of sorrow; some had brought tears of joy.

I tapped a pencil on the desk, and my mind replayed a call we had made more than fourteen years ago. First ring. Second ring. . . "We lost the baby." Voice subdued and sorrowful, Rick repeated the message several times to sisters and parents. For four years we had been trying. Now, for the second time in fifteen months, I had miscarried. Since childhood my goal was to be "a mommy, just like my mommy," and now I feared we would never have a child.

I had placed our name on an adoption list three years before but had heard nothing from the agency. Then, in the fall, seventeen months after my second miscarriage, the agency called. "Mrs. Sheppard, are you and your husband still interested in pursuing adoption?" After much prayer and discussion, we decided to go ahead. The home study took several months, and the following spring I received another call at work. "Mrs. Sheppard, I'm happy to tell you that you've been approved to adopt. We should have a newborn baby for you within a few months."

So close, we came so close to adopting, and then we received another call. "Rick, the bishop's cabinet has decided to appoint you to pastor a church in the southern part of the state. It's a small town about 140 miles away." Fearing the worst, we made the next call to the adoption agency and told the social worker our news. Her answer was not what we wanted to hear. "I'm sorry, but that part of the state is outside our jurisdiction. We'll have to transfer your name to another agency. The decision will be up to them, but you may have to wait at least another year."

Two miscarriages, and now this, I thought. *Our baby is close by and waiting to be born; only now he or she won't be our baby. Another lucky couple will suddenly become parents—and we just lost a third child.*

For the past four years I had carried a business card in my purse. The card carried the name of Dr. Behrman, one of the country's best fertility specialists. His number represented our final hope, but I had never called for an appointment. As we prepared to move, I pulled out the number and decided to call and set up our first consultation.

Dr. Behrman looked at us across his massive desk, while we sat nervously waiting for his opinion. "I've reviewed your records, Mrs. Sheppard, and I believe you have a hormonal imbalance—one that is easily treated." Several tests proved the doctor's theory right, and I started on progesterone supplements. But months went by and nothing happened. I began to question God's love for me. My faith was being tested, and it was proving weak.

One day Rick gave me a tape of Ann Kiemel Anderson speaking about "God's perfect timing" in her life. Thinking of my own doubts and fears, I found myself praying, "God, forgive my impatience. Please bless the baby that is to be ours, whether by birth or adoption. Guard his or her life from the moment of conception. Please help me wait with patience instead of despair."

For the first time in years, I felt at peace. I left the problem in God's hands for the next six months. In the meantime, Dr. Behrman added Clomid to my monthly regimen of progesterone supplements. At the phone's first ring, I snatched it up with trembling fingers. "Mrs. Sheppard?" Dr. Behrman's nurse sounded excited. "Your test is positive!"

I called my sister that night, ecstatic. I had waited years to make this call. Voice light and breathless, I prolonged the moment. "Are you sitting down?"

The months passed slowly. An ultrasound showed that the baby was fine. I enjoyed every kick and hiccup and took pride in my huge stomach. My water broke a few days before my due date. When I didn't go into labor, the doctor decided to perform a C-section rather than induce.

As he delivered Christine in November of 1982, he exclaimed, "The Lord was looking out for you!" Extensively wrapped up in her cord, she might have been strangled during a regular delivery. As she lustily protested her arrival in the brightly lit surgical room, Rick and I cried tears of joy—and relief. She was beautiful, healthy, and had red hair like mine! Phones rang in five states that afternoon with our miraculous news.

Knowing that we wanted to have another child, our obstetrician advised us not to wait. "It might take several years," he said, "and you are thirty-three. Go ahead and try again." Christine was just learning to walk when I called my sister again. "Are you sitting down?"

I had no complications during the second pregnancy. Scott, chubby and red-haired, was born in August of 1984. Every night on my way to bed, I checked on both sleeping children and prayed beside their cribs. "Lord, I am so grateful. Thank You."

Just after Scott entered second grade, I passed my forty-second birthday, feeling that my life was at loose ends. I tried to explain my feelings to a friend at lunch one day. "My part-time job is dwindling to a few hours a week. Somehow I feel next year is going to bring big changes. . . ."

Third ring. Fourth ring. My sister finally answered, bringing me quickly out of my reflection. "Hi," I said, my tone deceptively casual. "Are you sitting down?"

Laura was born in June of 1993—six days after our twenty-second wedding anniversary—a beautiful, dimpled baby with red hair like her brother and sister.

Our plans are not always God's plans. Our timing is not always God's timing. But His ways are perfect, and His gifts are infinitely good.

Sweet as Strawberries

by Carol Russell, Fort Scott, Kansas

"What are they doing?" I asked as Bob and I drove up the lane of my in-laws' farm. Dad drove the tractor slowly through the garden, pulling the large wooden farm wagon, and Mom shoveled something out of it.

"They're putting chicken manure on the strawberries," Bob said.

"How disgusting!" I declared. Bob laughed at me as he got out of the car.

Bob and I waved at them, then sat on the back porch steps while they finished their task. Laurie Ann, our two-year-old, began playing with the cats that had wandered up from the barn. I watched Bob's folks as they worked and thought about how little I knew about the farm and growing things. I was a city girl. Every time we came to the farm, I learned something new.

"Hi, you two," Dad said as he came across the yard. "Bob, I'm glad you're here. I need you to look at that tractor. I think I have a problem."

As Dad and Bob walked off, Mom bent down and stole a kiss from her granddaughter. Pulling off her gloves and sitting next to me on the steps, she sighed. "That's hard on old backs."

"I don't see how you do it," I said. "I just can't imagine standing in that wagon, shoveling that stuff."

"Well, it isn't my favorite job, and it certainly isn't the nicest, but all jobs can't be nice and smell good. It's still an important part of growing things. If we want good sturdy plants and want them to produce the best fruit, then we have to care for them.

"It starts with planting. Then we must weed and water them. Then they have to be nourished. That includes putting fertilizer on them. It will make the largest and sweetest berries."

"Thanks, but I think I'll just use sugar on my strawberries."

Mom laughed and said, "It's work, but the fruit we have in the end is worth it. You two go on in the house. I have to put away a few things and then I'll be in."

Later, as Mom was placing glasses of milk on the table, she asked her next question: "Well, how are things going?" This sent me into a long discourse of my trials and tribulations.

"That old wringer washer is broken again. We need an automatic, but the money just isn't there. I'm not sure it will last through another baby. I guess Bob will just have to fix it again," I said. Mom sliced two large pieces of bread from her homemade loaf. She began to toast the bread.

"The cost of Laurie's medicine went up again. Every time I have that prescription refilled, the cost goes up." She set the plate of toast on the table and walked to the refrigerator.

I lifted Laurie, put her into the high chair, and continued my complaining. "They changed Bob's hours at work. He's still the

21

early morning man at the station, but now he has two hours in the morning when he comes home and then has to go back. It sure has messed up our schedule." Mom took out a bowl of strawberry preserves and placed it on the table. We said grace and then began to enjoy our snack.

"I know what the Bible says," I continued. "I know what Matthew 6 says. God tells us that He watches the birds and cares for the lilies of the field. I know He loves and cares for us and that we shouldn't worry about tomorrow and about 'things.' It's hard, Mom. The harder we try, the harder it gets."

Thoughtfully, Mom placed a spoonful of preserves on the corner of her toast. "Maybe you and Bob are God's fruit," she said. "Maybe God is just putting fertilizer on His strawberries."

I never looked at strawberries—or trials—the same again.

The Greatest Soldier of All
by Patty Smith Hall, Hiram, Georgia

I saw him staring at me. He was a simple man. Sprigs of snowy white hair peeked out from beneath a dirty ball cap, framing a wrinkled face that had weathered a lifetime of storms. Wearing worn blue jeans and a button-up shirt that had seen better days, he was probably someone's father or grandfather, stopping in the magazine aisle for the newest puzzle books. But right now, he was staring at what I had in my hands. A photo essay on Pearl Harbor.

Being a child of the 1960s, the surprise attack that had drawn the United States into World War II was just a history lesson to me. But in this man's eyes, I saw memories of a time and place so real I could have reached out and touched them. I had to talk to him.

"Nice book, isn't it?" I opened the ensuing conversation.

The muscles in his throat moved, and for one brief moment, I felt ashamed for disturbing him. Then he spoke.

"I was there. Not for the attack," he added. He was a boy of eleven or twelve when the Japanese bombed Hawaii. He remembered the call to arms. The boys of Paulding County bravely marching to war. Stars hung in windows in remembrance of those who didn't make it back.

The attack affected him, and nine years later, he decided to join the marines. He shyly glanced at me. "I'd always been in church, saved when I was a young boy. But the service changed me, and I slid away from the Lord. Until I got to 'Pearl.' "

His orders came in. After a brief layover in Hawaii, he was being shipped to Korea to fight in a new conflict. Scared about what lay ahead, he decided to go see Battleship Row, particularly the entombed *Arizona*. Standing where so many had died, he watched as the infamous drops of oil rose to the surface. So many lives lost for the sake of freedom.

"And then, the Lord spoke to me in a quiet, still voice," he said. "He reminded me that one day the oil would run out and people could forget what happened there. But His Son shed drops of blood for my freedom that will last for all eternity."

The man gave his life back to the Lord that day, sure that no matter what happened in Korea, his everlasting freedom was secure. The old man shyly tipped his cap and shuffled away.

A lump formed in my throat as I gazed at the book in my hands, my fingertips caressing the laminated cover. So many young lives lost for the cause of freedom. One battle fought for our eternal deliverance. The nameless man had changed my textbook view of Pearl Harbor. Never again would it be just another documentary on the History Channel, but a constant reminder to give thanks for the men and women who serve our country every day. And to give wholehearted praise to the loving Warrior who battled the gates of hell to ensure my liberty from death.

For Christ truly is the greatest Soldier of all.

Getting Out of God's Way
by Barbara Curtis, Petaluma, California

Christine's shriek whipped into the room, slicing into my phone call midsentence.

"Barbara! Your car's rolling down the hill!"

Throwing down the receiver, I spun and raced down the hall. As if something had picked me up, shaken me, and booted me into a more focused dimension, I could see only the door at the end of the hall, hear only the pulse surging in my ears.

Seconds slowed and separated, like drops from a leaky faucet. Grabbing the only emergency cord I could, I begged, "Oh, God, dear God, please let the car be empty."

Moments ago, I had been leaving Christine's office, my toddler in my arms, my oldest son by my side. At the door, we had taken extra time for Jonathan to wave bye-bye. When the phone rang, Christine had turned back inside. The parking lot gravel was crunching under my feet when she appeared again at the door to say my husband was on the phone.

"Honey, will you put him in his car seat? I'll be right back." I turned to Joshua, eleven, who was everyone's right-hand man. Christine had asked him to come to physical therapy today to distract

Jonathan from the discomfort and tedium of his workout.

"Sure, Mom," Joshua said. I put his brother into his arms. At three, Jonathan was still too wobbly to negotiate the rocky parking lot safely. Down's syndrome meant his physical as well as his mental development was delayed. But for his family, his cute little face spelled courage and perseverance.

Why had my husband called that day? Neither of us can remember. He only recalls my cry of dismay and the sound of the phone clattering onto the floor. Then my screams.

"No! Oh no! Oh, God, please, no!"

The car wasn't empty. Through the windshield, I could see the top of Jonathan's blond head framed by his car seat. He was being carried backward down the sloping driveway toward the two-lane road below. On the other side of the road was a thirty-foot drop to the San Francisco Bay.

"Oh, Lord, not here, not now," I pleaded. Moments from Jonathan's brief but difficult life flashed through my memory. I could hear the beeps of the monitors in the ICU, see the tangle of cords and wires from the limp body, feel the tug on my stomach when the doctors prepared us for the worst. So many times we had been through these things, with so many people praying for our special little boy. And, one by one, God had healed him of his frailties. For the past year he had been so healthy we had actually begun to relax.

Could God really choose to take him now, after all He'd seen us through?

Not if my son Joshua could help it. Horrified, I saw him behind the car, straining his ninety-five pounds against the ton of metal grinding him backward. Running awkwardly in reverse as the car picked up speed, he was on the verge of being crushed any second. I couldn't lose two sons!

"Joshua, let go! Get away from the car!" I screamed. Christine was screaming, too. Even as we pleaded with him, I understood my son's heart. He always took responsibility. Everything within him would rage against giving up the battle to save his brother.

I screamed again, "Joshua! Obey me! Let go!"

At last he jumped away from the car. As Joshua let go, Christine and I stopped screaming. The quiet was eerie. The moment hung poised like the last drop of water from the faucet. The car seemed to hesitate, the rear wheels to shift. Now the car was moving at an angle toward the edge of the driveway, losing momentum, grinding to a halt. Almost gracefully, it came to rest against an old and faithful-looking tree.

Bolting for the car, flinging open the door, I found Jonathan unhurt but bewildered—he had never been in a moving car all by himself before! Catching sight of Joshua right behind me, Jonathan grinned and stretched his arms wide—his way of saying, "Life—what an adventure!"

I've been behind a rolling car. I've tried to pit my puny weight against circumstances that were way too big for me to handle. Perhaps that's why I understood Joshua's reaction all too well.

"Mom, all I could think of was that I couldn't let him die," Joshua told me later.

"All I could think of. . ." That's me all over, willing to sacrifice everything for some good purpose. And ever overestimating my indispensability. Even if I know I need God's help, don't I often think He needs mine as well? Don't I often act as though God can accomplish the supernatural only if I stay involved?

Maybe sometimes He is just waiting for me to get out of the way and let Him take care of things before I get myself hurt. Maybe He'd like to do something truly miraculous, something I'd always remember—something I couldn't take credit for myself. Maybe He'd like me to be more like Jonathan, just going along for the ride, a little worried, perhaps, but remembering I'm in good hands and ready for the rescue.

I hadn't put my car in Park. That little bit of carelessness almost cost me two sons. But God chose instead to teach me a lesson about His mercy and His might. He gave me a picture I will never forget—one son trying to avert disaster, letting go in desperation, and being saved. The second, powerless and utterly dependent on God's own outcome.

Because Jonathan is who he is, he might always keep that sweet simplicity. And I will ever be learning from his triumphant trust as he stretches out his arms and smiles. "Life— what an adventure!"

Looking for God at Charles de Gaulle Airport

by Cheryl Norwood, Canton, Georgia

There we were, in Charles de Gaulle Airport, Paris, France, Sunday morning, 6:00 a.m., bone-tired from an eight-hour flight from our home in the Atlanta, Georgia, area. The seats on the plane had been very comfortable and the service great, but we had been one row away from the lavatories, a popular place on a long flight. We would just doze off and then hear the door open or close or have someone stumble into us. We never got more than a few minutes' uninterrupted sleep.

In the airport, we were as helpless as children. We knew only a few phrases in French. We almost turned this trip down due to that very fact but then decided we needed a break. We both worked full-time outside of the home in high-stress positions. In addition, both our families had been going through health crises and struggles. Maybe a free trip to France would help renew us!

Our enthusiasm for this wonderful gift began to drain with each passing moment as we waited in the airport terminal for our train. We had thought to exchange dollars for francs before we left, but at 6:00 a.m., nothing was open anyway. We were thirsty, but all the vending machines took only coins. We tried several times to get change from other airport inhabitants, but none understood our limited French or cared enough to be of any help. We found a bench to sit on, but it was hard, shiny, slick sheet metal. My gabardine slacks made it difficult to sit comfortably because I kept sliding off the bench onto the floor! I finally piled up our entire set of luggage in front of me as a barricade.

Miserable and concerned that this was a sign of what the rest of our week would be like, I began to pray. "Please, God, help it to get better. Please help Mike have a good time. Right now things don't look too good, and we are tired and hungry and anxious. Give us Your peace." When I opened my eyes, I noticed Mike had a big, goofy grin on his face. "What's so funny?" I asked.

He answered, "Listen to the PA system. Can you hear what they're playing?"

I strained to hear the music. Ray Charles was singing "Georgia on My Mind."

Slowly the same goofy grin slipped across my face. God had heard my feeble little prayer even before I prayed it, and this was His answer. Georgia was on Ray Charles's mind, and two Georgians were on God's mind. Suddenly we both felt better, and we both were filled with renewed hope and faith that the next week would be wonderful. It's great to be on God's mind!

Go Fish!

by Linda Parker, Windermere, Florida

I was a single young mother with two beautiful daughters. And daily I faced the challenge of being the mom, the dad, the breadwinner, the plumber, the painter, the gardener, and the auto mechanic.

So in recurring intervals, when my two daughters got that longing look in their beautiful eyes, I experienced all the pangs of failed parenthood. A child should have a pet. A pet means companionship, responsibility, and that special bonding.

Fish were always my solution—a compromise, my default position, and the backup plan. We couldn't afford a dog or a cat.

Plus, my plate was already full. How could I manage to be responsible for one more living creature on this earth? But when a little girl really wants a white kitten so badly that she names her fish "Fluffy," that fish carries extraordinary responsibility as a pet.

Early one unremarkable Saturday morning after Fluffy had been swimming in circles in a glass bowl on the kitchen counter for many months, I noticed he wasn't looking his glowing best. His usual deep maroon color was gray-tinged and he lingered near the bottom of the bowl. *Uh-oh,* I thought, dreading the presumed inevitable.

I changed the water in his small container. I carefully replaced the seashells and plastic mermaids that Fluffy's young decorators had lovingly added to his abode. "Come on, Fluff," I coaxed. "Carrie adores you." Fluffy, as usual, was noncommittal.

I heard two sets of bare feet come tramping down the stairs. I knew from experience that before they got the cereal box, even before they came to look for me, seven-year-old Carrie would go to the counter and check on Fluffy, and little sister, Amanda, like a faithful sidekick, would be right behind.

Three, two, one, I counted silently. "Mo-o-om!" Carrie called out from the kitchen. "Mom, something is wrong with Fluffy!" Her voice quivered.

"Well, maybe he'll be all right," I reassured. "I changed his water," I added, as if that might have promoted a miracle cure.

As the morning passed, it seemed apparent that Fluffy was passing, too. By late afternoon his color was entirely gray. His usual rounded form seemed strangely flattened. *Can a fish be dehydrated?* I wondered.

Carrie and Amanda checked on their patient frequently. As the worst seemed unavoidable, I tried to prepare them. "You know, Fluffy has been with us a long time in fish years."

"And he is going to be with us until we are old, isn't he, Mommy?" Amanda contributed cheerfully.

"Well, honey, pets like fish and turtles don't always live as long as people."

"Mommy, there are Galapagos turtles that live forever. I saw it on TV. And there are catfish that are as old as you!" Amanda continued, emphasizing the word "old" a bit more than I liked. Amanda was such a bright, helpful child.

"Oh, sweetie, all I'm saying is that it may be time for Fluffy to go to live in heaven. We know he'll be so happy and healthy there."

As if on cue, Fluffy took a turn for the worse. He now floated diagonally, almost at the surface of the water. His gills appeared motionless. I had to admit that Fluff had never charmed me quite as he had Carrie and Amanda. Now that he looked like a canned sardine, I felt quite sorry for the little guy.

"You know, girls, maybe the kind thing would be to go ahead and take Fluffy out of his bowl. He's dying; he looks terrible. I think he's almost gone, and we don't want to see him suffer."

Tears began to roll silently down Amanda's pudgy cheeks. Carrie was very quiet, and then she spoke. "No, Mom, let's not bury him yet."

"But, Carrie, he's. . ." I wanted to say "gross" but fumbled for a kinder word. "He's miserable."

"No," said Carrie, "let's give him a little more time."

That afternoon Carrie was very low-key. By bedtime, poor old Fluffy was floating sideways on top of the water. His splendid red color was gone. He gave no sign of life.

"Girls," I began, "I think it is time to. . ."

"No, Mom!" said Carrie authoritatively. "Fluffy is going to be fine." Her tone was insistent.

"Honey," I spoke gently, "Fluffy has gone to heaven. Let's

get a nice little box and we can bury him under the big tree in the backyard."

"Mom, Fluffy is going to get well," my faithful daughter insisted once again.

"Carrie, I am sorry, but I think Fluffy is dead."

Amanda looked first at me, then her big sister. For a change, she was speechless. I looked at Carrie's silently pleading face, and against all logical judgment, I said, "Okay, sweetie, we'll leave Fluffy in his bowl until morning."

I did not have to face my morning alarm clock. Carrie's excited voice woke me just before daylight. "Mom, come see Fluffy!" she shouted. *Oh, dear,* I thought, rubbing my eyes and fumbling for my slippers. Fluffy's bowl had been my last stop just before bedtime. His gray, lifeless body had floated on its side on the surface of the water.

"Carrie. . . ," I stopped my sentence. Words weren't forming in my brain, much less my mouth. In his little bowl, our fish, Fluffy, was swimming—and swimming vigorously! His color was deep red and his shape was firm and plump again. I couldn't think what to say. If Carrie had not been a seven-year-old in flannel pajamas, I would have believed that she had been to the pet shop and purchased a replacement Fluffy.

"What happened?" I asked as Carrie and Amanda jumped about and giggled.

"I prayed," Carrie answered matter-of-factly.

"What did you say in your prayer?" I asked incredulously, as

I held Fluffy's bowl up to the light, still not accepting what I was seeing.

Carrie's look, as she was already getting out her cereal bowl, reflected what a dumb grown-up question she thought I was asking.

"Mom, I just prayed for God to make Fluffy better!"

"Well, God certainly listened to your prayer, Carrie."

"Sure, Mom, that's what He does," she responded, quite matter-of-factly.

After several days I gave up checking on Fluffy in his bowl every few minutes, as if I anticipated at any time to discover him floating, colorless, on the surface of the water again. Good old Fluff lived another two happy and healthy years with us. When he finally died, Carrie and Amanda buried him sadly but with acceptance. They wrote "Fluffy" on a small board and placed it over his grave. I added the name "Lazarus."

Fluffy-Lazarus lived his small life large. His recovery and Carrie's uncomplicated faith became a symbol in our family of what the power of prayer, fortified by sincere conviction and earnest hope, can accomplish.

The Wall

by Iris E. May, Ulster, Pennsylvania

Bill kicked the pebble, sending it onto the next lawn. He glowered, murmured, and swore under his breath. "Why don't they have signs telling you how to get there? It's not supposed to be a secret."

We had walked for an hour up and down Pennsylvania Avenue in Washington, D.C.

I pointed. "Let's try over there."

Finally, we found the line leading to "The Wall." It wound its way back at least a quarter-mile. The closer we came, the more agitated Bill became. A park volunteer handed him a directory. He skimmed through it.

"How am I supposed to find anyone with this stupid thing?"

"Let's ask someone to help us," I suggested.

He glared at me. Then he blurted, "How am I ever going to find my unit? Why couldn't they list them by units?" He ran his hand though his hair and kicked an imaginary stone.

"Honey, what's the matter?"

He almost roared. "I can't remember their names! How can I find them if I can't remember their names?"

I laid my hand on his arm. "I'm sorry."

"Why can't I remember? I ate with them, slept with them, and held some while they died." He drew a deep breath. "Now I can't remember their names." He hung his head.

My strong, sensitive husband was crying. I ached with pain for him. A gentleman, several people ahead of us, dropped back and stood beside Bill, though he never looked directly at him. "When were you there?"

Bill glanced up. "1969."

"I was '68 to '69. You been here before?"

"No. You?" Bill quizzed.

"Yeah, many times."

His shoulders slumped forward and his hands slipped into his baggy coat. He shuffled his feet, staring at the ground. Then he looked over the park, his eyes blank.

Bill's face held the same look.

"I can see their faces. I can hear them screaming with fear and pain even in my sleep," the man said. He wiped his hand over his eyes. "Sometimes I come here and stay all day. They don't seem so loud from here. Like I'm closer and they don't have to yell so loud, you know?"

"Can you remember their names?" Bill questioned.

"Only a few. Their eyes, their broken bodies, but not their names."

"I thought it was only me. I feel terrible. I'd hope someone would remember my name, but I can't remember theirs."

"Yeah, me neither. While I was over there, I got so I would

not learn names. It didn't hurt so much for some unknown to die, but a friend? I lost too many and became hard on purpose."

"Me, too." Bill nodded. "I'd just learn a name, a little about his family, and he'd get shot." Neither man asked or volunteered names here either.

When we stood beside the wall, Bill reached out and traced names with his finger. "I wonder if he was one. . . ."

We worked our way around the corner. Suddenly Bill exclaimed, "Here they are! This was the squad that almost got wiped out. We came in from a two-day patrol and waved to them on their way back out." He choked. "I never saw most of them again."

"Gomez, Hector, Smith, Smith. . ." He read the names, touching each with his finger. He knelt by the spot and put his head against the wall. When he stood, he turned to me and started talking.

"We called this one Small Fox because he crawled in the tiniest holes."

He'd point to another name and tell me what he remembered. Mostly nicknames, or hair color, or a strong southern accent. One had dried squid sent from Hawaii. The buried memories now rolled from Bill's mind.

I stood silently. Listening. Praying God would turn Bill's mourning into gladness, sorrow into comfort and joy. He'd held twenty-six years of grief. Maybe now the hatred would be released. With God's help he would finally be at peace.

That visit to the wall did free him. I watched my dear husband make a dramatic turn from hate to hope, from horror to healing. Today he freely talks about his experience in Vietnam. God gave him peace.

A Lesson on Prayer
by Cheryl A. Paden, Fremont, Nebraska

"These two molars will have to be pulled," the orthodontist said. I listened carefully to his explanation of the latest plans for my son Isaac's teeth. I was acutely aware of the look of fear on Isaac's face at the mention of pulling teeth. I knew he didn't want to go through that again. However, I made the appointment with the dentist. In two weeks, the teeth would come out.

Every day Isaac begged not to have the teeth removed. He came up with all sorts of other options. Having gone through the same thing as a child myself, I strongly sympathized with him. It was necessary, though, and I could see no way out of it for him.

As we drove to the dentist's office on the day of the dreaded appointment, I glanced into the rearview mirror. My son was in the backseat with his head bowed and his hands folded in prayer. He must have sensed me looking at him. "I'm praying to not have my teeth pulled," he explained to me.

I was heartsick. I knew how disappointed he would be. Concern that his faith in prayer would now be lessened troubled me. I had no words of comfort, so I just drove.

In the dentist's office, the nurse took Isaac back to the procedure room. I sat in the waiting room with a heavy heart, knowing how frightened he was feeling.

In a few minutes, Dr. Mike came out to me. "I really don't know why these two teeth need to be removed. I'd like to call your orthodontist and discuss it with him." I was stunned. Sure enough, one phone call to the orthodontist confirmed it. The teeth could be left to fall out naturally.

I left the office with a very happy little boy. I could only shake my head in amazement. How had I forgotten the basic truth that God listens and answers even our simplest prayers?

That day we both learned a lesson about the power of prayer. One learned with the faith of a child and one through doubt. Next time I'll try to have the faith of a child. And I won't miss another opportunity to pray with my son.

In the Spirit
by Sara Jordan, Limestone, Maine

"Hey, where are your lights?" the neighbor called from her front porch next door when I stepped out of our house to get the mail.

I turned in her direction. "What?"

"Your Christmas lights and decorations. You usually have them up Thanksgiving weekend!"

I glanced down at the mail I was gathering and shrugged before answering. "I guess we're just slow this year," I finally said.

She nodded and smiled, and I stepped back into the house, sighing as I closed the front door. I dropped the mail on the entry table and plopped down in the easy chair near the door, closing my eyes for a minute. It had been a long, frustrating day, and I was ready to put my feet up for a few minutes before my husband, Dave, got home from work. Nothing at work had gone right for me, which was par for the course lately. I had been feeling restless and discontented for a while, and the impending Christmas season had something to do with it.

The neighbor was right—we usually went all out for Christmas starting Thanksgiving weekend. Dave would string the lights around the windows and front porch, I would decorate with window

42

decals and homemade ornaments, and we would always get a live tree from the lot down the street. I loved the Christmas spirit, the coziness and softness it lent to everyday living. Yet here we were entering the second week of December without the usual fanfare.

"Oh, Lord, forgive me for my lack of enthusiasm," I began to pray. "It's just that this time last year we were sure that we'd have a baby by this Christmas. We've been trying for over five years now. I know You're taking good care of the two babies we lost to miscarriage, but we still miss them. We started the adoption process last year led by Your divine guidance, we're sure. It wasn't supposed to take this long. Why has everything gone wrong? And now the thought of another childless Christmas, a season so devoted to the innocence of childhood, is breaking me. On top of that, I have two relatives and five friends who are either pregnant or have newborns. I try to be happy for them. I need Your strength, Jesus. Please restore the joy of my salvation and give me hope again. In Your name I pray. Amen."

By the time I was done, tears were streaming down my cheeks. *I'm so tired,* I thought. *How can I keep going? How can I face that attic full of boxes of decorations, all filled with dreams but no children yet?*

After dinner that evening I approached the subject with Dave, telling him about my prayer.

"Let's just turn up the Christmas music, dig our heels in, and put up the decorations," he suggested.

I reluctantly agreed, knowing it was as good a time as any. We drove down the street to the tree lot and slogged through the mud to choose a tree. My heart wasn't in it, but we finally found one after searching row after row. I had to admit the smell of pine was comforting.

"What's that?" Dave asked, when we returned home to see a cardboard box on the porch with a card attached.

We hurried inside and I tore open the card to read it. I saw immediately that it was my mother's handwriting. "It's from Mom," I told Dave as I began to read the note. "She must've dropped it off while we were getting the tree."

I read the note aloud: "To remind you of the true meaning of Christmas so that you will celebrate in your heart. This is for all the future traditions you will have with your children. Love, Mom and Dad."

Dave had opened the box and begun to pull out the protective packing. I dropped to my knees on the floor beside him. Tears flowed again when I realized what was in the box.

It was a Nativity scene—a wooden stable, three wise men, a shepherd, Mary, Joseph, and a little baby Jesus. It wasn't just any Nativity scene, however. It was the one my parents had bought the first year they were married and kept for the past thirty years. It had been my job to set up the Nativity every year as I was growing up while my parents told me the story of Jesus' birth. It was a cherished tradition that my parents had passed along to me in the hopes that I would share it with my own children. They still had hope for grandchildren. In fact, they firmly believed that it would happen in God's perfect timing, even if I couldn't understand the plan completely. Through this gift, they had stepped out in faith. How could I do any less?

I picked up the baby Jesus figure, cradling it in the palm of my hand. I wondered how Mary must have felt giving birth to the Savior, the very Son of God. Christmas was not about my expectations. Christmas was about celebrating the birth of Jesus, and in my own distractions, I had forgotten. I didn't need external things to "get in the spirit"; the Spirit was already eternally in me.

I smiled through my tears as I told Dave, "God has answered my prayer in a big way today. I've got to call Mom and Dad; then let's put up those decorations!"

That night as we went to bed in a home sparkling with Christmas spirit and homemade decorations, I turned to a favorite scripture: "Those who know your name will trust in you, for you, Lord, have never forsaken those who seek you" (Psalm 9:10).

Milk Money
by Jo Upton, Jonesboro, Georgia

No one could ever say my dad was a slacker. As soon as he finished his time in the navy, he went right to work loading airplanes for a major airline in our area. He and Mom were married before he turned twenty, and within ten years he was supporting a family of five on a tight budget.

As children we never felt deprived, because this was the '50s, a much simpler time. People didn't wear designer clothes or hundred-dollar shoes, at least not in the little neighborhood where we lived. My two younger sisters and I wore homemade dresses and worked hard to take care of our "school shoes," making sure they lasted until spring. That was when Dad bought our Easter shoes, the only other pair we would get for the year.

Mom and Dad worked as a team, because without living wisely, we couldn't have made it. Dad always worked overtime when it was offered and filled in for anyone taking sick leave or vacations. There were two things he was determined to give his family: a small but comfortable home and regular meals, something he made sure we never lacked. We had only one car, but there was never a question about having enough groceries.

Dad had grown up during the Depression, and sometimes having an egg or a cup of sugar was a luxury no one could afford. That may have been the reason he felt it was worth any price to make sure we had good, nutritious meals. He made it his top priority, using the two checks he received each month to buy groceries first. Then, when the money ran low (as it usually did), he didn't have to worry about his family going hungry.

This same caring nature carried over into making sure we had proper diets at school, too. He often did without things he needed himself to make sure we had money for hot lunches and that my first-grade sister had milk money. The younger children had a morning break each day and could buy a cup of milk for a snack. Dad felt it was important because she was a fragile child, often sick and on medications.

The abundance of medical bills sometimes caused money to be scarce at our house. Dad was a responsible man, never allowing any debt to accumulate. Because he paid on time and in full, a few unexpected doctor visits could quite literally leave him penniless.

It was during one of these extreme money shortages that we all learned a lesson about God's provision.

Dad worked the night shift, going to work just before midnight and arriving home the next morning before we left for school. It was his routine to give my sister the money for her milk as he kissed her good-bye. The milk cost three cents a cup, but sometimes those were the only three pennies he had in his pocket. Of course, he never let us know at the time it was his last bit of change; he would just dig into his pocket in an exaggerated way to make us giggle, then scoop out the three copper coins to place lovingly into the hand of my tiny sister. He was totally dependable; she knew every day she would have milk when it was served. It was one of those small gestures that make little girls feel secure and dads feel like heroes.

One morning, however, he left work tired and defeated. There were a few days left until payday, and the money was gone. . .not nearly gone, but totally. The last straw was when he felt inside his pocket to assure himself that he had milk money but couldn't find any change. His spirit crumbled. The one thing he wanted more than anything was to provide for his family. How could he go home and tell his little daughter that she couldn't have milk with the other children because he didn't have three pennies?

His heart cried out to God for help that morning as he walked to his parked car. Within seconds, he felt impressed to look down at the ground below him. He did so almost involuntarily, and there on the pavement directly in his path was a gleaming dime! He reached down for it, giving thanks quietly, and tucked it deep inside his uniform pocket.

This would be milk money for the remainder of the week, enough to last until his next paycheck.

When Dad arrived home, there was an extra spring in his step and a glow to his countenance as he reached inside his pocket for milk money. My sister's eyes were wide with delight when he handed her a dime instead of the customary pennies and told her to pay for the rest of the week in advance.

At just the right time, God the Father had given my dad exactly what he needed to provide for his child. He knew, and we later learned, that we had experienced a true-life miracle.

From Numbers to Nelly

by Mary J. Dixon Lebeau, Woodbury, New Jersey

Her name was Nelly Adler. For a little while, it was my name, too.

Six million Jews, and millions of others, were executed during the Holocaust. They were beaten, tortured, gassed—methodically murdered. For years they were faceless casualties, but recent efforts have put faces to those numbers, letting us personalize the loss—and learn from it.

At the United States Holocaust Memorial Museum in Washington, D.C., as visitors check in at the door, they receive an identification card, a passport into the past. That's how I became Nelly Adler. I read the front of the card: "For the dead and the living we must bear witness." I opened the cover to gaze into long-ago eyes.

Nelly was born February 28, 1930, in Liege, Belgium. *So she celebrated a birthday a day before mine,* I thought, feeling vaguely connected to the dark-eyed girl in the oversized bonnet. She was the youngest of three daughters born to Czechoslovakian parents, and her family was a Jewish family living in a primarily Catholic town. Though her parents spoke Yiddish, Nelly grew up speaking French like her friends.

As I traveled the exhibit floors, I learned more about life for

Nelly and her family during the Nazi regime. The terror hit home first as synagogues and businesses were razed, windows smashed, school doors shut. Then the Adlers and other families were sent to ghettos, where everyone, including twelve-year-old Nelly, was forced to work in sewing factories or at hard labor.

According to my identification card, Nelly's father was in a hospital, seriously ill, when the family was awakened at 5:00 a.m. by the Gestapo's angry shouts.

"Where is your father?" they demanded.

"He's in the hospital," the sleepy girl answered.

"Liar!" one official yelled, slapping Nelly's face.

The household was arrested. They never saw Mr. Adler again.

I wandered through the rooms that depicted horrors of the concentration camps. I stood in the small, windowless wooden train car where Jews and others were packed together and transported to the camps. Although I knew I was safe, I began to understand the fear. I wondered how Nelly sustained her faith, knowing that prayer would be my only comfort on this train.

"We also exult in our tribulations," I reminded myself, whispering the Bible verse. When these people exited the train, the Gestapo took their belongings. The Adlers weren't suspicious, since this had happened when they were forced into the ghetto. Then Mrs. Adler and her daughters were taken to a large showering area and were told to remove their clothing.

"You must be showered to kill the lice," they were told.

On the last page of the identification card in the Holocaust museum, you read of your fate. On that camp visit, everyone in my party was liberated.

Everyone except Nelly.

With her mother and sisters, she and others waited for the water to hit. But the water never came. Instead, the room filled with lethal gas. Nelly Adler died in Auschwitz on May 21, 1944, at fourteen years old.

The horror didn't stop there. After death, the bodies were brought where gold fillings were removed from their teeth and their hair was cut to sell for wigs. Then, ten at a time, the bodies were cremated.

As I left the area, feeling stunned at the fate I shared with Nelly, I completed the Bible verse I had whispered earlier, "We also exult in our tribulations, knowing that tribulation brings about perseverance; and perseverance, proven character; and proven character, hope" (Romans 5:3–4 NASB). I know that hope will continue, even in the dark days. Even when we can't understand the horror, we must hope—and remember.

So I will remember not only the six million Jews and millions of others, but also the sixty thousand Vietnam casualties, the 168 deaths from Oklahoma City, and those thousands stolen from us in September 2001. All these moments in history have turned countless hearts toward God.

Most of all, I'll forever remember one little girl. Her name was Nelly Adler. For a little while, I shared her name.

His Little Girl

by Barbara Curtis, Petaluma, California

I remember the day my dad left. He knelt and hugged me and cried. The skimpy dress of a five-year-old girl couldn't protect me from the chill that gathered around my arms and legs. The scratchy, tickly whiskers—would I feel them no more? The arms that felt so safe—would they be gone forever?

What would it be like not to have a father?

The years to come provided harsh answers to those questions. Mine was not a carefree childhood. Shuffled with two brothers between foster homes, relatives, and—when things worked out—my mother, I toughed out the hard times.

My innocence gave way early on to a cynic's worldview: Don't depend on anyone, and no one will disappoint you.

As anyone without a father will agree, the loss doesn't end when you grow up. The scars are like the glossy, too-tight skin that grows over a healing wound. Beneath the protective cover lies too much tenderness.

For the longest time, I didn't know about the tenderness. I tended the gloss—taking control of my future, acquiring a good education, rising above the pattern of my family's past. I guess you might say with no one to believe in, I learned to believe in myself.

Only when this unsustainable strategy dropped me down-and-out—and more alone than ever—did I finally face my fatherlessness.

So it was in my thirties—when I sensed what was missing was spiritual—that I finally launched a search for God. For someone like me, the New Age movement held enormous appeal. Here I could wander into nooks and crannies, borrowing this and that to construct an image of God that meshed with my own deficiencies. Crippled by the lack of a real father in my life, seeing God only as some remote and impersonal force, my hope was that through understanding, I could appropriate the force—recognizing "God within me"—then manipulate it to find happiness.

With my eyes on the ground, happiness was as high as I could aim my sight. I wouldn't have thought to seek His love.

And yet how amazingly unconditional and enduring His love remained for me. No matter how I misunderstood Him, He continued to understand me. How patiently He waited as I wandered—for seven more years protecting me from harm, continuing to draw me nearer, gradually softening my heart.

My husband helped to soften me—though I never could have told him then. Watching him father our children was like peeking through a frosted pane into a warm and cozy home within.

Although seeing my children experience a happy childhood was the next best thing to having one myself, how I wished sometimes to climb inside and receive that kind of love myself.

Oh, how ready I was the moment I first heard God was my

Father! How easy it was to believe He loved me, had a plan for my life, and through Jesus Christ would have a relationship with me. Of course I wanted a Father!

At last, I was Someone's little girl!

To this day, ten years later, I cannot approach God intellectually, only as a child. Yet He has never asked me to do more. With no reservations, I feel His love: "Though my father and mother forsake me, the Lord will receive me" (Psalm 27:10). Is it not a miracle that someone who missed an earthly father's love can be healed to receive the love of the heavenly Father? But isn't He Jehovah, the God who heals?

The greatest privilege of all is to call Him Abba, Father.

According to *Vine's Expository Dictionary of New Testament Words*, " 'Abba' is a word framed by the lips of infants and betokens unreasoning trust. *Father* expresses an intelligent apprehension of the relationship. The two together express the love and intelligent confidence of a child."

I remember once, before he left, my father carried me home in his arms as blood gushed from a jagged cut on my foot. I was four and frightened, hoping that my father could take care of me. But though that day he bound and stopped the bleeding, no earthly father could have healed the wounded heart he later left behind.

That hurt cried out for the love of a heavenly Father.

No matter my age, I will always be His grateful little girl—trusting, dependent, and filled with faith in the arms that will never let me go.

The Guardian Angel

by Renie Szilak Burghardt, Doniphan, Missouri

The first time I saw my guardian angel, he was pointing a machine gun at us. It was early spring of 1945, and my grandparents and I had just emerged from a bunker where we had spent a terror-filled night.

I was nine years old then and lived in Hungary; World War II was playing havoc with our lives. My grandparents, who were raising me, and I had been on the road in our horse-drawn wagon for many months, searching for a safe place. We had left behind the village of our birth in the Bacska region because Tito and his Communist partisans (guerillas) were closing in on the region.

By day, we'd move swiftly, ready to jump out and take cover in a ditch if warplanes were approaching. By night, we camped with other refuge-seekers along the roadside. I usually lay bundled up in my feather bed in the back of the wagon, cradling my cat. War was almost all I had known during my nine years; there seemed to be no safe place to be found.

After the Christmas of 1944, when we were almost killed in a bombing in the city we were in at the time, Grandfather decided that a rural area would be safer. So we moved to one in upper

Hungary and settled in a small house that had an old cemetery as its neighbor. Here, Grandfather, with the help of some distant neighbors, built a bunker in a flat area behind the house. And on that early spring day in 1945, we had spent the entire night in the bunker.

Warplanes buzzed, tanks thundered, and bombs exploded over our heads all night, but finally at dawn everything grew deathly still. Grandfather decided that it would be safe to go back to our house. Cautiously, we crept out into the light of early dawn and headed toward the house. The brush crackled under our feet as we walked past the cemetery. I shivered, holding on to my cat tightly. He had spent the night in the bunker with us.

Suddenly there was a rustle in the bushes just ahead. Two men jumped out and pointed machine guns directly at us.

"Stoi!" one of the men shouted. Since we were from an area where both Serbian and Hungarian had been spoken, we knew the word meant "Stop!"

"Russians!" Grandfather whispered. "Stand very still, and keep quiet."

But I was already running after my cat. She had leaped out of my arms when the soldier shouted, so I darted between the soldiers and scooped her up. The younger of the two soldiers, tall and dark-haired, approached me. I cringed, holding Paprika against my chest. The soldier reached out and petted her.

"I have a little girl about your age back in Russia, and she has a cat just like this one," he said, gently tugging one of my blond braids. "And she has long braids, too, just like you." I looked up into a pair of kind brown eyes, and my fear vanished. Grandfather and Grandmother sighed in relief.

Well, both soldiers came back to the house with us and shared our meager breakfast. We found out from them that the Soviet occupation of Hungary was in progress.

Many atrocities occurred in our area, as well as throughout our country in the following months, but because the young Russian soldier took a liking to me, we were spared. He came to visit often, bringing little treats along for Paprika and me, and always talked longingly of his own little girl. I loved his visits, yet I was terrified of the Russians in general. Then one day, almost a year later, he had some news.

"I've been transferred to another area, *malka* ["little one"], so I won't be able to come and visit anymore. But I have a gift for you," he said, taking something out of his pocket. It was a necklace with a beautiful turquoise Russian Orthodox cross on it. He placed it around my neck. "You wear this at all times, *malka*. God will protect you from harm." I hugged him tightly and then watched him drive away, tears welling in my eyes.

World War II was over, but for the people of Hungary, a life of bondage was at hand. Many men who had been involved in politics or deemed undesirable were being rounded up by the secret police, never to be seen again. Not long after, the dreaded knock on the door came to our small house. They came to take my grandfather away. Fortunately, Grandfather managed to sneak out through a window and go into hiding. Then it was just Grandma and me, trying to survive as best we could. When my cat died, life truly seemed unbearable. Sometimes I would finger the cross my Russian guardian angel had given me, and wonder where he was. Was he back home with his own daughter? Did he remember me?

The time passed in a haze of anxiety and depression. Then in the fall of 1947, a man came to get us in the middle of the night. He said he would take us to the Austrian border and we'd be reunited with my grandfather. We traveled all night to a place where the ethnic Germans of Hungary were being loaded into transport trucks and expelled from Hungary. The man gave us counterfeit papers so we could all cross the border to freedom. When we arrived, a weary-looking man with a thick, scraggly beard and a knit cap pulled low over his forehead was waiting for us.

"Grandpa!" I cried out, rushing into his arms. It was so wonderful to see him again.

Then we walked toward the transport truck loaded with dozens of people and got on, fake papers in hand. I knew if we were found out, it would mean Grandpa would get hauled off to prison, and worse yet, he might even be executed. I glanced toward the Russian soldiers who were coming closer to inspect the papers, and I prayed to God for Him to keep us safe.

Then I looked up as a guard boarded the truck. I caught my breath.

"Grandpa," I whispered. "Look, it's my soldier! He is checking this truck." I wanted to leap up and run to him, but Grandpa shushed me cautiously.

"Maybe he won't recognize us," he whispered, pulling the knit cap further down his forehead.

Then my soldier was before us. My grandfather handed over our papers without looking up. I leaned closer and put my hand protectively on his shoulder while I peered cautiously at the Russian, hoping to see the old kind sparkle in his eyes. But he was intent on the papers, his expression grave. I didn't dare to breathe. At last he handed the papers back to Grandpa.

"Everything is in order in this vehicle," he announced. Then, winking at me, he got down, and in an instant the truck began to move on. I looked over my shoulder and caught my guardian angel's eye.

"Thank you." I mouthed the words, holding up the cross hanging around my neck. He nodded discreetly, then quickly turned and walked away. As we crossed the border to safety, we all breathed a sigh of relief.

Although we had suffered much sadness during the war, one blessing will always stay with me: the memory of a kind soldier who turned my fear to faith and showed me that God's compassion can be found anywhere.

A Matter of Perspective
by Carmen Leal, Naples, Florida

I don't remember what we were arguing about on January 28, 1986, at 6:37:53.444 a.m. Hawaiian time, but I know my husband and I were again at odds. We'd had more bad times than good in eight years of marriage. In a counseling session, my pastor asked what we fought about. I retorted, "What don't we fight about?" We agreed on nothing from finances to children to values. A new Christian, I knew arguing with my husband wouldn't please God or solve our problems. But that didn't stop me from quarreling with as much fervor as my nonbelieving spouse.

As we drove over the Pali Highway for our daily commute from Kailua to Honolulu, the radio was tuned to the news station. I heard only snatches of news stories as I focused on making my point—the right point, of course.

As we entered the tunnel, a special live report interrupted the normal program. But we lost transmission. We bickered so intently about what could be so important that when we emerged from the tunnel and the static cleared, we almost missed the announcement. The *Challenger* had exploded.

The beauty of the majestic emerald velvet Koolau Mountains

and the brilliance of the aqua waters mocked my feelings of confusion and despair. My unhappiness with my husband, my marriage, and my life no longer mattered. An unspoken truce silenced us for the rest of the commute. We listened to the broadcast as we inched our way down Bishop Street before turning onto Kapiolani. My tears fell as I saw clusters of brightly dressed businesspeople obviously discussing the news in front of office buildings and open spaces. I offered up a prayer for the astronauts and their families.

It was anything but business as usual that morning as employees and management crowded into the conference room to view televised images of a mission gone so horribly wrong. Murmurs of disbelief mingled with sobs set the tone, as we watched the two solid rocket boosters corkscrew across the sky, trailing brilliant white plumes of frozen vapor. In mounting horror we watched as the ship broke up and fell blazing into the sea.

Television monitors at the spaceport showed paramedics parachuting into the sea. A rescue force was dispatched to see what might be done. We watched the men unload the remains of the seven recovered from the Atlantic Ocean.

Eventually I went back to my office until it was time for the evening commute. As we inched through rush-hour traffic, my husband and I listened to updates about the *Challenger* and its six astronauts and one teacher. Ellison Onizuka, the first Japanese-American astronaut, was from Hawaii. Hawaii's newscasters repeatedly mentioned his name and birthplace.

A contemplative mood replaced the tense atmosphere of the morning ride. As we approached the nursery school to pick up our sons, I thought about Ellison's wife, Lorna, and their two children. Suddenly my marriage didn't seem so disastrous.

The children's laughter greeted me as I walked into Sunshine Preschool. My active, healthy sons ran to me, chattering. In comparison, two children in Hawaii that day would never again see their father. A wife would never get to make up after an argument. Spurred by thoughts of an intact family, and grateful that I could still work out our problems, I thanked God as I held each child by a hand and walked them to the car.

The state of my marriage that day had felt hopeless. My husband and I each needed to change things. Before that day, I had been trying to solve every problem instead of trusting God for guidance, comfort, and hope. Trusting God meant relinquishing the safe yet faulty methods I had devised to get through each day. Now I needed to act out my faith. That meant loving my husband as God had outlined in 1 Corinthians 13.

The *Challenger* wasn't a catalyst that healed my marriage, but it drew me closer to God and taught me to trust Him with my entire life. It also changed my perspective about what constitutes a disaster, and it precipitated a major U-turn in my life. That day I realized that as long as I have faith, I have hope. And as long as there's hope, nothing is a disaster.

Burning Bushes

by Wendy Dunham, Brockport, New York

One afternoon as I was looking through my hope chest, I came across a letter tucked inside a yellowed envelope that I had written as a child. On the front of the envelope was written, "To God." As I opened it, I was overwhelmed by God's goodness to me. Now, twenty-four years later, I still have the childlike faith that burned in my heart when I wrote this letter:

Dear God,

I feel so confused, but I'm glad I can talk to You. I don't know what to do about my dad; he doesn't believe in You. I'm sorry, God. I wish he did. He says the stories from the Bible aren't true and that there's no way they could have happened. Like the story about Jonah and the whale. . . He said it is a fable because no one could live in a whale for three days. And he said that Moses didn't lift his rod and separate the Red Sea, because the laws of physics make it impossible. He's heard about the burning bush, but he says that if it were on fire, it would have been burned up, and that I should know bushes don't talk! What should I do? I love You, God, and I believe the Bible is

true. But what about my dad? I always thought he knew
everything, but now I'm not so sure. Can You help?

Love, Wendy

At the time I wrote that letter, my mother was a "silent" believer. She felt "being quiet" about her faith would help keep peace in our home. Several days had passed before I discovered my mother had found the letter and written a response:

Dear Wendy,

I found your letter. Please forgive me—I couldn't help but read it. I hope you understand. I'm sorry about your dad. I wish he believed, too. I know how confusing all of this must be for you. You see, sometimes adults reason too much with their minds and not enough with their hearts. Your dad reasons with his mind. He has chosen his disbelief, but don't let that change yours. Be strong in your faith, and continue to seek God. You have been saved by faith, a gift God has given you. If you look in your Bible, at Mark 10:15, you will read: "I tell you the truth, anyone who will not receive the kingdom of God like a little child will never enter it." And yes, Wendy, burning bushes do talk!

Love, Mom

Now, late in life, my dad has come to know the Lord with a childlike faith. Bible "fables" have become facts. Jonah is no longer a fictitious character but a real man for whom God had a plan. The Red Sea no longer represents the laws of physics but a miraculous passageway for the Israelites. And as for burning bushes, just the other day I overheard him reading from Exodus to his grandchildren: "And when Moses saw the flames and realized the bush did not burn up, he went over to see it. Then God called to him from within the bush, 'Moses! Moses!' And Moses said, 'Here I am.' 'Do not come any closer,' God said. 'Take off your sandals, for the place you are standing is holy ground. . . .' "

Joy filled my heart as I heard my father share his childlike faith with my own children. God is still a God of miracles! "Though you have not seen him, you love him; and even though you do not see him now, you believe in him and are filled with an inexpressible and glorious joy" (1 Peter 1:8).

The Rules of Life
by Linda Parker, Windermere, Florida

Andrea played by the rules. She always played by the rules. Andrea's world was a neat, tidy package.

At seventeen, she had carefully evaluated the scholarships she had been offered for four years of paid college education to prepare her to teach music. She sought advice from her high school guidance counselor, discussed her options with the church music director, and made her final decision by considering her parents' preferences as well as the cost of commuting. After mailing in the commitment letter, there was nothing left to do but stand back and bask in the praise for making such mature, sensible choices.

Her life followed an orderly progression. Four years of college, National Music Honor Society, and, three weeks before graduation, she received an offer to teach in Hardinsburg Elementary School.

At Hardinsburg Elementary School, she was quickly recognized as a first-rate teacher. Every summer she returned to the university, each time taking on a new area of specialized study.

Andrea learned methods of music therapy in order to use music to unlock doors of silence and isolation in emotionally disturbed children. She took course work in physical therapy so she could help children with physical challenges participate in Hardinsburg's beginner band. Her final summer in graduate school was spent mastering sign language so that she could bring deaf and hearing-impaired children into the music classroom for the first time. Andrea was not far from sainthood in the eyes of her students, their parents, and the Hardinsburg Elementary School administration.

When a young attorney opened a new practice in town, no one was surprised that he, too, would take notice of Andrea. Nor were folks surprised when, a few months later, Mike and Andrea proceeded with a proper plan—marriage, wait two well-planned years, then start a family.

Andrea, true to form, managed her pregnancy with textbook precision. Milk became her drink of choice, jogging was replaced with yoga and stretching, and she played classical music for her unborn child.

Early one rainy morning, just before Thanksgiving, Mike and Andrea became the parents of a tiny baby girl with delicate features. Ann Marie had beautiful brown curls, large blue eyes framed by dark lashes, and ten elegant piano-player's fingers. She also had permanent brain damage—cause unknown. How could this have happened?

While Mike worked overtime, Andrea alternately wept, worried, and shook her fist at God in her frustration. "How could He do this to me?" she ranted. *I paid my dues in advance,* she thought resentfully, *with my service to handicapped children.*

Christmas was soon only days away. Andrea and Ann Marie rarely left the house. Unable to postpone them any longer, Andrea had some unavoidable holiday preparations to complete, even for the small-scale celebration Mike and Andrea had planned.

Ann Marie wore a warm pink bunting as Andrea loaded her into the stroller for their first shopping trip. Every store display they passed was alive with moving figures, musical sounds, and twinkling lights, all designed to draw the delight of children. The elaborate decorations seemed to be designed for the sole purpose of reminding Andrea of God's unfair decision to deprive her of a healthy baby and to burden her life with the care of a handicapped child.

After pushing the stroller through the crowd of shoppers, Andrea took a few minutes in the ladies' room to stop her tears. As she wept in the privacy of a toilet stall, she heard a woman speaking to a child. It was a happy conversation, filled with the anticipation Christmas brings to a child's chatter. Andrea felt another sharp pang of jealousy for what this other mother and daughter obviously shared.

Pulling herself together, Andrea parked the stroller near the counter so she could wash her hands before she and Ann Marie returned to the crowded mall. The woman and her daughter continued to talk enthusiastically about their upcoming holiday plans as they washed their hands. Andrea's heart pricked with true envy as she watched them, but she stopped short when she saw the child's face for the first time.

The little girl in front of her was probably not more than eleven or twelve. She had long dark hair, almost as curly as Ann Marie's, and she wore a red cap turned at an impish angle. She also had the unmistakable features that identify Down's syndrome.

Andrea realized she was staring openly at the pair. She struggled for something to say, a way to explain her rudeness. Finally, she stammered, "I'm sorry to stare. You two just sound so happy." It was an awkward moment.

The mother could have reacted indignantly, but sometimes empathy prevails. In the instant that she peeked into the stroller, the woman remembered being Andrea, being a new mother engulfed in hurt and misdirected rage.

"You have a beautiful baby," she said.

Andrea nodded, but she could not think what to say.

"You know, God only picks special mothers to have special children," the stranger added, and with a "Merry Christmas!" she and her daughter went on their way.

Special mothers? Special children? Suddenly it did not matter that Andrea's world was no longer the same neat, tidy package. It was the surprise and wonder of a gift from God, and it took a stranger in the ladies' room to point that out to her. This was the blessed task for which God had prepared her. How could she have been so blind?

Andrea scooped Ann Marie into her arms and held her tightly. "You," she said to the sleepy, blinking bundle, "are my greatest blessing. God entrusted you to me." And looking heavenward, she said, "Thank You, God, for opening my eyes, thank You for sending Your Son, and thank You for sending my daughter." Laughing, she added, "And thank You for sending us into the ladies' room!"

When No Jobs Existed
by Jennifer Smith-Morris, Valdosta, Georgia

In the heart of the Depression, lanky Howard, with his twinkling blue eyes and wavy brown hair, had already learned to live by his wits. His mother had left the family of ten when Howard was eight. His father couldn't care for all ten children, so at nine, Howard left home and lived with relatives, getting work wherever he could. By the time he was eighteen, he knew how to work hard, stretch a dollar, and find hope in a bleak situation.

Howard was my granddad. I knew him as a man with sparse gray hair but with the same lanky frame and twinkling blue eyes. He told me he'd always believed that God would provide. That was his faith: Granddad always asked for just enough—not too much and not too little, and his faith carried him time and again.

In 1934, Granddad was living in Wisconsin, where, like the rest of the country, there were no jobs. "Everywhere you looked, men were hungry and out of work," he'd say. Then the corners of his eyes would crease with a smile. "But I always managed to get some dinner."

Sometimes he would go to the diner that offered a Dime Plate dinner. He recalled, "I didn't even have the dime for the Dime Plate." He asked if he could wash dishes or scrub the grill for a plate of food.

He roamed the countryside. Sometimes he'd split wood at a farm, then knock on the door and ask if he could do anything else to earn a meal. Sometimes he'd ask permission to sleep in the barn. "A little straw under my head, and I was pretty cozy for the night."

Men all over the country stood in lines, pleaded with factory owners, and struggled to avoid starvation and homelessness. Granddad heard a rumor that the local tannery needed workers. He started going each day to see if they had any jobs. Dozens had the same idea. "The room was packed. Just packed full of men."

Every day the foreman would squeeze out of the office door and announce that they had no jobs. He would return to the office and slam the door as the men filed out, heads low. Day after day Granddad left without work. This frustration must have deflated many. But it strengthened Granddad's resolve.

One day, weeks later, Granddad again heard the foreman make his announcement and again watched the room clear. Then he walked up to the office door.

"I figured the way to get some notice was to go on in there." So he stepped inside the dimly lit office and asked the foreman, "Did you really mean there aren't any jobs?"

With colorful language, the foreman assured Granddad that indeed no jobs existed. Granddad left smiling, returning the next morning to see if work was available. He never felt defeated. The obstacles he'd faced in his young life strengthened his survivor's spirit.

Many years later, Granddad imparted this same spirit to his family. God will provide, he believed. God is faithful through all generations, just as the psalm says. It was a matter of figuring out how the Lord would provide, and Granddad took it as a challenge to find out.

After several more daily visits, Granddad set off for the tannery as usual, ready to work, ready to go hungry, ready to see God work. But that morning, the tannery had an opening. Desperate men packed the room more tightly than ever. The office door swung open, and the foreman stood on a bucket and held up one finger. Shouts and arms raised as he peered at the crowd.

Granddad went into action, twisting through the crowd, aiming for the office door. He kept his head high, watching the foreman. The foreman surveyed the sea of faces, then pointed his finger at my granddad, yelling, "I want you."

And because of his tenacity, perseverance, hope, and faith that God would indeed turn things around, my granddad got that job even though no jobs existed.

A Simple Act of Faith

by Gerald Eisman, Sarasota, Florida

As I read the announcement of her death, memories flooded back. Her name was Sister Ana Marie, and she was one of the strictest teachers in St. Theresa's Academy, a primary school for good Catholic children and incorrigibles who couldn't function in a public school setting. I guess I was one of the latter.

Considering the reputation I brought along from the public system, I found the easiest way to ease pressures put on me by the Sisters was to volunteer for chores, which I did—often. Except that when I volunteered, it was usually my dad and sometimes my mom who wound up doing the work. I just reaped the rewards.

One hot Friday in early June, as we were packing our books and pads to take home for the weekend, Sister Ana Marie (aka Sister Torquemada) asked, "I was wondering, is there anyone here who might get a parent to drive me to the train station next Saturday? I must be there promptly at 7:00 a.m."

Another chance to ingratiate myself and score some more brownie points. My hand shot up. I waved it back and forth while punctuating the action with grunts and a broad grin. "Are you sure your parents won't mind, Mr. Armani?"

"No, ma'am," I said. "My dad will be happy to do it."

"Do what?" my dad exploded when I told him what he'd been volunteered for. "Have you lost your senses? I work seventy hours a week and spend Saturday cleaning and shopping, and you tell Sister that I can take her to the train? That station is twenty-odd miles from here, not counting the distance from our house to St. Theresa's." He fumed at me for a good half hour before he relented and agreed to do it.

At five o'clock on Saturday, I was rudely awakened by Dad. "Up and dressed," he rasped at me. "I want you to know what it feels like to sacrifice your morning off." He pulled the sheet from my body, letting the cold morning air touch my warm skin. I yelped, and he smiled. "Very good," he said through clenched teeth. "Very good. The lesson begins."

We picked up Sister Ana Marie "Torquemada" and began the trip to the train station, two towns east of ours. "A very good morning to you, Sister," my dad greeted her, despite what he was feeling.

"If that be God's pleasure," was her terse answer. She took her place in the backseat, placed her one small bag on the seat beside her, and folded her arms across her chest. Staring forward, lips compressed in her usual dour manner, she closed down all paths of communication.

"And where will you be going?" Dad inquired of the good Sister.

"Cleveland," was her succinct response. Out of the corner of my eye, I caught the glare Dad tossed in my direction. His head began to shake back and forth. Boy, oh boy, I was in for it when we got home. I was convinced of that. The rest of the trip was made in silence, Dad scowling at the road, me sweating, and Sister staring straight ahead.

When we reached the station, Sister took a seat on a wooden bench at the station house. Dad politely carried her bag over and placed it beside her.

"Have you gotten your ticket?" he asked as politely as he could.

"Not as yet."

"Well, if you will give me your money, I'll purchase it for you."

Sister looked up at Dad. "I have no money."

"No money?" Dad sputtered. "How do you intend to buy a ticket to Cleveland without money?"

"God will purchase my ticket for me," Sister said, confidence embedded in every syllable.

"God? God?" Dad shook his head as if to dislodge an unwanted insect. "Good luck, Sister," he grunted, then returned to the car with me trailing after him. He brought the engine to life, jammed the machine into gear with a loud grinding noise, and released the clutch. We lurched ahead.

"God's gonna buy her a ticket," he muttered to no one. "Ridiculous!" We drove for several blocks before he looked, or rather glowered, at me. He pulled the car to a stop at the curb.

"Did you know about this?"

"No, sir," I answered honestly. "I sure didn't."

"Do you honestly think anyone will buy her a ticket?"

I hesitated a moment before answering. "I would if I had money," I told him. I reached into my pocket and produced two crumpled one-dollar bills and held them out to him. We looked at each other. "Really. I would. You told me once, 'Never turn your back on someone less fortunate than you.' Then you said, 'There but for the grace of God go I.' " We stared at each other some more.

With a suddenness that Dad was noted for, he wrenched the wheel, turned the car around, and headed toward the station. We found Sister Ana Marie seated exactly where we left her. I stood next to the bench while Dad strode to the ticket window. He turned and glared at me again. Sister seemed not to notice.

"Round-trip to Cleveland," I heard him tell the ticket master. He paid for the trip, returned to the bench, and did something I had never seen him do before. He removed his hat and sat next to Sister as he handed her the ticket.

"I guess you were right about God and the ticket," he said. "Have a safe trip, Sister."

It was a day of wonders, because then I saw Sister do something I had never seen *her* do before. She smiled. "I surely thank you, Mr. Armani. You are as good a man as your son is a good boy. God will reward you for this kindness." Sister then resumed her severe look and stared straight ahead.

On the way home, I stole a glance at Dad and caught him with a big grin on his face. He noticed me looking, tousled my hair, and grinned even wider. "God will reward me, eh? Sister is right, you know, but her timing is off. He already rewarded me when He gave me you. You are a good boy."

I was stunned. I was convinced he never noticed me, and based on that childish observation, I'd made a conscious decision to fight him every minute of my life. When I looked into his eyes, I saw that he meant it! He meant every word.

Dad passed away a few years after that incident, far too young as far as I was concerned. However, I had discovered an amazing truth. My dad was really a very kind man, and he loved me. Dad's remaining years with me were filled with wonder and discovery and understanding.

My eternal thanks to you, Sister Ana Marie, and your simple act of faith. It returned me to my father, or perhaps my father to me, giving us the best years of our life together.

Pride and Prejudice

by Lynn Roaten Terrell, Wichita, Kansas

I cranked open the little side window in the front seat and savored the fresh air blowing onto my warm cheeks. The front seat was usually reserved for grownups. If no other adults were in the car, my seven-year-old brother got to ride up front with Mamma. But today, it was just Mamma and me in the car. I felt very special.

I watched out the little window as we sped from the relative prosperity of southern Tennessee to the hovelled communities of northern Mississippi. We soon pulled into a driveway—a path, really—that led to an unpainted shack. A yard full of laughing children with beautiful dark golden skin and curly ribboned hair scampered to greet us. A cute little girl was even wearing a blouse like I used to have. I was sure we would find lots more in common if we were given the chance to talk.

I ached to jump out of the car and play with them. But then my heart raced with excitement as my special friend, LoAnna, kissed them all good-bye and hurried toward our car.

Usually she rode the bus in, but today we got to pick her up. She often fixed soup and grilled cheese sandwiches for my brother and me for lunch, and she patiently cared for our baby sister. One time, using a hoe, she fought off a nest of lizards she found behind my brother's bed. She didn't complain when the bird egg broke in my sun-suit pocket. LoAnna even let me play in the doghouse with our beagle, and she generously warned me three times before turning my many misdeeds over to my mother for discipline. She was the only grownup I was allowed to call by her first name.

As LoAnna joined us, I scrambled into the backseat, following the family rule that adults always sat up front. LoAnna stood awkwardly as my mother caught my eye.

"You need to get back here in the front seat with me," she ordered.

"You mean in the front seat with the two of you?" I was sure I had heard wrong.

"No, up front. . .just with me."

LoAnna smiled her gentle, knowing smile as she nodded her okay. Confused, I crawled out of the back of the car. I held the seat forward for her as she nestled herself amid the Popsicle sticks and apple cores that garnished the backseat.

I didn't understand. Mamma obviously thought LoAnna was good enough to care for her children. So I couldn't figure out whether Mamma thought LoAnna wasn't smart enough to be around grownups or whether LoAnna might have done something wrong and wasn't allowed to sit up front.

I will never forget the ride home. I was humiliated by the fact that I, a child, had taken the place of honor away from a grownup who had earned my utmost love and respect—for a few dollars a day, plus bus fare. As punishment, I closed the little side window that gave me such joy. The front seat had abruptly lost its allure. It was years before I understood this event.

That was 1955. During the sixties, I was protected from much of the racial turmoil as I attended a small college in northern Mississippi. As Easter 1968 approached, I looked forward to relaxing at my grandparents' house in my hometown. Then, just before I was to leave, an intense emotion filled the air at my college.

"What's all the excitement about?" I asked my friends as we sat in the auditorium for the chapel service.

"Dr. Martin Luther King Jr. was assassinated in Memphis. I hear they're sending riot squads to control the protesters."

The dean took the podium. "I am sure you have all heard about the shooting of Dr. Martin Luther King Jr. Most of you have to travel to Memphis this week, but curfews are in place due to rioting. As you know, the campus is usually closed over Easter," he continued.

"I bet they'll cancel our holiday," I moaned.

"So if any of you are afraid to go home, we will let you stay in the dorms."

Despite the warning, I caught the bus. Passengers discussed the shooting until the bus picked up passengers at the black college. After that, we rode in tangible silence.

When my grandfather picked me up at the bus stop, I didn't recognize the city I loved. The odor of burning trash hung in the air as protesters lit garbage dumps. And Memphis, once a clean city, was now strewn with rusting garbage cans overflowing with rotting food.

My uncle, who worked for the city, was assigned to guard a landfill. After curfew began for the city—and armed with a pass from the mayor's office—my aunt and I took dinner to him. We visited for several hours—hours that were palpable with the textures of fear.

Although it seems like only yesterday, a lot has changed since then. Cars no longer have those wonderful little side windows. Adults ride in the front seat and children sit in the back, secured by seat belts.

Prejudice has existed since the beginning of time, and as long as we have sinful natures, diversity will exist. Yet it is possible to make a turn toward God when we fill our hearts with God's love—a love that knows no color, no race, no creed. We have turned the corner toward change, but we still have a long way to go.

Because of those changes, children will never again have to try to analyze the parsed words of grownups as they're ordered to give their seats in the back to an adult. I didn't understand it then; and now, more than forty years later, I still don't understand it. Yet I will press onward and pray that in time our nation will be able to understand that powerful message of hope and healing that comes from treating hatred with love.

Sixty-Six Poinsettias

by Eva Marie Everson, Casselberry, Florida

"Sixty-six," my neighbor Maryse said. I'd just entered her front door to find her standing, emotionless, staring at the red, pink, and white poinsettias crowding the foyer and lining the hallway. I shivered in the chill that permeated the home—not so much from the December air but from the events of the past week. On December 2, 1987, Maryse's daughter Laura had been killed in an auto accident.

Having been neighbors for nearly a decade, we'd raised our six children together. Mine were as much a part of her home as hers were of mine. We even had special nicknames for the kids. I called twenty-year-old Laura "Laura Sue."

"What?" I asked.

"Sixty-six. Sixty-six poinsettias. Sixty-six reminders that my daughter is dead."

I'd never thought of the traditional flower-giving at funerals in such a way. I also couldn't imagine, nor begin to imagine, the agony my friend was experiencing. I did see that the flowers only seemed to add to her grief, though.

"Do you want me to take them somewhere?" I said softly.

"I can do that. I will do that."

"No," she said with a sudden jerk of her head. "I'll think of something."

A few hours later she called. "I know what I want to do. I want to do what Laura would have done. She loved the elderly. Remember how she used to bake cookies and take them to the nursing home?"

I remembered.

"I want to do what Laura would have done," she said again. "Are you and Jessie available Friday night?"

"Sure," I said. Jessica, my six-year-old, and Maryse's son Hayes were best friends.

Then she filled me in on the plan.

Friday evening, Maryse was armed with the poinsettias. Hayes and Jessica, dressed like Santa's elves, carried candy canes donated by Bob's Candy Company; a friend of Maryse's husband came dressed as Santa; and I toted a camcorder on my shoulder to record the evening. We entered the warm, anti-septic hallway of a nearby nursing home with a "Ho! Ho! Ho!" and a "Merry Christmas!" Tired, age-lined faces broke into childlike amusement and wonder, and their old, watery eyes beamed with excitement.

After acquiring permission, our festive little group made the rounds with Santa's joyful "Ho! Ho! Ho!" proclaiming our presence mirthfully at each room's doorway.

"Oh, little darlings! Little darlings!" The residents extended their arms, welcoming our little elves.

Greeting each resident by name (their names were on the doors), Maryse said, "Merry Christmas," and placed a poinsettia on the nearby bedside tables.

"Merry Christmas," they said. "You're so sweet! So sweet!"

I steadied the camera and peered into the lens through tears. This was the single most selfless act of love I had ever witnessed. My friend gave out of her grief. She took flowers commemorating her daughter's death and turned them into gifts of the season of hope, joy, and the ultimate gift of love.

I have no doubt that Laura stood next to her Lord and smiled at the five of us. It was exactly what she would have done.

Time of My Life
by Stephanie Welcher Buckley, Edmond, Oklahoma

"Teach a life-skills class in an inner-city school?" I asked during a staff meeting. "Why in the world would I do that?" As a single woman in my thirties, I had a comfortable workload and didn't want to add another job responsibility. Besides, what did I know about teaching? I had no interest in public education. I didn't even have children!

"As employees in the community health department, our mission is to make the city a healthier place to live," my boss explained.

How this goal would be accomplished by teaching a roomful of high school kids was beyond my comprehension. My duties as a community development specialist in an Oklahoma City hospital were mundane compared to the competitive career I'd had in journalism and broadcasting eleven years earlier. However, my job was simple, and the salary was excellent. I had traded challenges for security.

"The last thing I want to do is babysit twice a week," I complained to a coworker at lunch.

"Then make it easy on yourself," she suggested. "Have guest speakers come in and talk about topics like careers, managing money, nutrition. . . . We work with those kinds of people right here at the hospital."

That afternoon, I planned the curriculum and made a prospective speakers list. Rather than class assignments or home-work, I would base the student's grade on attendance, writing thank-you notes to classroom guests, and keeping a journal of the points they heard from each speaker. *The less work for me the better,* I thought.

When the day arrived for me to go to the classroom, I was nervous. Standing at the front of the class, I saw a sea of multi-cultural faces. They seemed so fragile, not at all like the images I had seen watching MTV. One boy's dyed red hair was tipped green; another sported large tattoos on his neck, ankle, shoul-ders, and forearms; and two pregnant girls sat together in the second row, their stomachs bulging behind the desks. *A class full of misfits,* I thought. But from somewhere inside myself, I heard a voice say, *"You've gotten as far off track as they are."*

As the semester wore on, I began to see the students as chil-dren in need of encouragement and acceptance. "You did an excellent job on this thank-you note, Maria," I praised the Hispanic girl with gang signs on her hands. "A whole page! Way to go!"

She smiled, pleased by the compliment. "I liked the way Ms. Daigle talked to us," Maria said. "Someday I want to be a counselor and help people like she does."

The speakers were making a difference for some students,

but I never imagined that I, too, would be changed by one of these lectures. Back at the office, my boss stopped at my doorway one day. "I booked a friend of mine for your class. He is one of our doctors and likes to encourage young people."

"There is a change in your syllabus," I said at our next week's session as a tall, handsome black man walked into the classroom. I introduced Dr. Johnny Grigg. He had grown up in poverty, but he used his physical ability as a football star to win a scholarship to college. Instead of playing professional sports, he focused on education and became a neonatal intensive care pediatrician. The students were mesmerized by the soft-spoken man in green surgical scrubs.

"Think of your life as the face of a clock. Most people live to be about eighty years old, so that would be the twelve o'clock position. You are almost twenty years old, and that puts you at three o'clock, so a quarter of your life is gone." This analogy seemed to hit home as the class listened thoughtfully to our speaker.

"None of you are here today by accident," he said, scanning the room, making eye contact with each student. Then he said something that reached to my core, just as it seemed to touch the class. "God has a purpose for your life." He paused to let this sink in and then continued. "One of my favorite Bible promises is found in Jeremiah 29:11: 'For I know the plans I have for you,' declares the Lord, 'plans to prosper you and not to harm you, plans to give you hope and a future.' "

I hadn't anticipated our guest would discuss spirituality, but it was soon evident this aspect was the very foundation of his life. . .and the kids were listening intently.

"God has a blueprint for us all. He wants us to discover our destiny through a relationship with Him," he confided. Dr. Grigg went on to explain the importance of making every day count. His presentation was filled with encouragement, support, and love. His eyes glowed with excitement as he said, "Choose wisely how you spend the time you have left." We all sat and listened, spellbound, until the buzzing of his beeper broke our somber trance. Dr. Grigg had to get back to the hospital, but he had left us all enough to think about for a lifetime.

On the way home, I realized the hands on my clock approached six! For all practical purposes, my life was half over. The dreams of a journalism and broadcasting career put aside, I had focused on a safe, uncomplicated, mediocre life.

That evening I prayed God would lead me to a career that glorified Him and fulfilled me. In my journal the next morning, I wrote about the regret of giving up on the gift God had given me—the ability and desire to write.

Although not a morning person, I began waking up at 5:00 a.m. to write before going to work. Almost daily I remembered the clock analogy and prayed about how to serve God through writing. Soon a concept for a book emerged. I felt energized by my passion. What a contrast from the lethargy and apathy I felt doing my job at the hospital.

Several months later I told a coworker about my writing routine and the lack of time I had to write. "They're going to have to fire me before I have enough time to finish that book," I joked. Twenty minutes later my boss called me into her office. A reduction in force caused me to lose my job! Just as Dr. Grigg had said, I suddenly realized God had a plan for me. The hospital's severance package allowed me to launch a career as a Christian communicator. I had time and money to follow God's plan.

Never again would I comb the want ads and accept an easy or meaningless way to make a living. No longer would I hide my talent and desire to write. Dr. Grigg's words reminded me that following God's direction would fulfill my destiny. The hands on the clock of my life warned that there was no more time to waste. Instead of regretting years wasted following my path instead of God's, I focus on Dr. Grigg's advice to "choose wisely how I spend the time I have left."

Today I am having the time of my life following God's plan and serving in a career that glorifies Him. Never again will I chart my own course.

A Dentist Made Me a Fighter Pilot
by Lowell "Duke" Embs, San Antonio, Texas

Two weeks before I graduated from the University of Illinois, the Korean War started. As soon as I got home from school, I went to the navy recruiting office in downtown Chicago. The place was packed, so I stood in line holding my birth certificate, college transcript, and social security card.

When I got to the head of the line, a guy with several stripes on the sleeve of his white jumper looked at me from behind a desk.

I paused and said, "I want to be a navy fighter pilot."

"Go out that door, turn left, and go to the first door on the right."

His eyes said, "Move," so I did. The first door on the right opened easily to a very large room containing at least two hundred guys my age in various stages of undress. For the next six hours, I became like them, answering more questions about my physical condition than I had ever had to answer before.

About 5:00 p.m., those of us who remained were told to come back the next day for more tests. These turned out to be IQ, psychological, and psychiatric evaluations.

At the end of those exercises, we were told we'd be notified whether we passed, and if we did when to report to Pensacola,

Florida, for fighter pilot training.

I was ecstatic when I learned I had passed, and each day that I waited for my orders grew longer than the last. My only comfort was the attention I received from the gals in town when I would tell them I was going to be a navy fighter pilot.

Five months after being accepted, while still awaiting my orders to Pensacola, I developed a toothache. Off to the family dentist. His office was a second-floor walk-up in an old building in Blue Island, a downscale suburb of South Chicago. Dr. Cibock didn't make appointments. You just showed up, signed in on a legal pad, and waited your turn. The space wasn't air-conditioned, and the doctor didn't use Novocain, so it was best to have a tooth problem in the colder months.

When I was finally seated in the dental chair with mouth open, Dr. Cibock said, "What's the problem?"

"This tooth hurts," I said, pointing to a lower molar. "I've gotta get it fixed before I go."

"Yep, you have some other cavities, too; where are you going?"

"Waiting to go to Pensacola to be a navy fighter pilot," I proudly said.

"Well then, we'll just fix this one and let the navy take care of the rest after you report in."

"Okay by me," I said.

And that's the way we parted. I was five dollars lighter but pleased my dentist was willing to hand me off to Uncle Sam for future care.

Four months later my orders arrived. They read something like this: Report to Naval Air Station Glenview, Ill., Building 21201 at 0800 on 1 June 1951, for processing to Naval Air Station Pensacola, Florida, as a Naval Air Cadet (NAVCAD).

Whoopee! In the navy at last. . . Well, almost.

The first thing that began after we all assembled was clothing removal—much like we'd experienced nine months previously. When I reminded one of the medics we'd already been down this road, he replied, "That was then; this is now." And the look that accompanied his statement clearly meant back talk was not allowed.

So I went along in silence until I was seated in the dental chair. The dentist was a full navy captain, probably about fifty. He poked, prodded, and pushed, finally saying, "Sorry, son, we can't take you in this man's navy."

"You can't what?" I said, leaping from the chair. "What do you mean?"

"We have strict medical prerequisites. You have too many cavities. You don't qualify for the NAVCAD program."

My world fell apart. I was ready to try anything as I pleaded, "Listen, Doctor, sir, ever since I was accepted nine months ago, I've told every pretty girl who'd listen I was going to fly the navy's fastest and newest jets. If you don't let me in, I'll be destroyed. I'll never be able to show my face at home. . .never."

"Sorry, Embs, you have too many cavities."

"I'll get them fixed," I practically begged.

"A dentist would have to stay up all night."

"I know one who will."

"What's his name?"

"Dr. Cibock."

"Really?"

"Please, Doctor, sir, I've gotta get to Pensacola."

"Okay, meet me here tomorrow morning at eight with those teeth fixed, and you can go."

It was 4:45 p.m. Next door was a building that said "Ships Store." I ran inside and headed straight to the cash register where I traded two dollar bills for twenty dimes. Out of the corner of my eye, I spotted a telephone booth. Inside hung a phone book for the North Chicago suburbs, both white and yellow pages.

"Okay, God, You're on—help me out here," I prayed as I flipped to *D* for dentists and started calling.

My pitch was simple: "I need an appointment *right now* to get some cavities filled so I can go to Pensacola, Florida, in the morning to learn to be a navy fighter pilot."

I got laughed at, hung up on, and apologized to—but on the fourteenth call, I hit pay dirt. The dentist had been in the navy and told me to get to his office as soon as I could!

I called a cab, and thirty minutes later he pulled to the curb. The dentist smiled as I bolted in. I grinned back. His assistant had left for the day, so it was just the two of us. Fortunately for me, and how I thanked God for it, he had the latest in equipment, high-speed drills, water-circulating devices, and the best thing of all—Novocain.

For three solid hours, he drilled and filled. When it was over, he told me he'd repaired seventeen surfaces. At three bucks a crack, that came to $51.

The cab fare back to NAS Glenview was another $5, leaving me with $37 from the $100 I'd started with that morning. I found my room in the B.O.Q. where we were billeted for the night and set my travel alarm for 6:00 a.m. My aching jaw didn't impair my sleep, and the next thing I heard was the buzz of my clock.

At 7:30 I was waiting for the navy dental office to open. When it did, I went in and sat erect in the waiting room. The doctor arrived and gave me a half nod.

Soon my name was called, and I went where the enlisted man pointed. The doctor with four stripes stood beside the chair; I sat down and he said, "Open up."

I did.

"Well, I'll be," he said with a smile. "Go catch the train with the rest of your pals, and good luck, son."

Later that night, as I listened to the sounds of the rails, I thought of the dentist who, quite literally, saved my career. Without his help, my entire life would have been different. I owed my future to an unselfish man, and I silently thanked the good Lord for sending me the dentist who had what it took to make me a navy fighter pilot—a warm heart, a sense of giving, power tools, and Novocain.

E-mail from God

by Linda Parker, Windermere, Florida

I would like to think I always hear God's voice when He speaks to me, but the truth is, I've been known to miss it. Now and then, caught up in worry and earthbound timelines, I have simply failed to see His answers. Recognizing this, I sometimes whisper quietly, "Please, dear God, don't set fire to the shrubbery," lest He feel the need to get my attention through a burning bush. Goodness knows, as a working single mom, I have had enough problems keeping my yard tidy without the landscaping bursting into flames.

For many years I have supported my children by writing—stories, articles, advertising—whatever words I can sell. Writing gives a working mom a career pursuit from home, saves a small fortune in child care costs, and lightens the extra load of guilt that single mothers all seem to carry heavily upon their backs.

Besides, I love to write. I cannot "not write." The fact that people give me money to do it is both amazing to me and sometimes quite incidental.

This does not mean that the flow of money and the bills to be paid always come in synchronized harmony. My children were teenagers before I realized that they thought the words to the

Twenty-third Psalm included, "Yea, though I walk through the valley of the shadow of debt."

And it was during one of these shadowy, wandering times, with writing assignments few and far between, that God might have resorted to E-mail to get my attention.

Four hundred sixty-four dollars. I needed it before the end of the month to pay the bills. Expenses were increasing, and my earnings struggled to keep up with my two growing girls, groceries, and an aging car.

So I did what writers do. I submitted outlines for books I thought were sure to be best-sellers and proposals for stories I thought would be "must reads." Editors did not share my enthusiasm. Before, in between, and around being a writer and a mom, I prayed.

I prayed, I stated my case, and sometimes I just downright begged. Was God hearing me? I questioned. Did He understand about compound interest and late fees? Time was running out, my faith was getting shaky, and I had overdue payments.

On the second week of that particularly uncertain month, I threw caution to the wind. I couldn't pay the utility bill, but I could sure spring for two Happy Meals after church and become one popular mom.

We ate our Sunday dinner on the playground. Then while my children squealed and giggled their way through a yellow plastic tunnel shaped like French fries, I spent a precious dollar and a half on the Sunday paper. My purpose: to search the want ads.

There it was! A job for a freelance writer! I'd never heard of the company, and I wasn't sure if I understood the job description, but I knew as I read the ad that I would apply as soon as I got home. As directed, I sent my resume to their E-mail address.

The next morning, I checked my mailbox. "You've got mail." The company had sent me their seven-page application. Two days later, I had interviewed twice by phone, when Chris, my new editor in cyberspace, offered me the job.

We had discussed everything but my paycheck when Chris began to add numbers aloud. Would I submit two short articles each month for two hundred dollars apiece? Absolutely! Would it be all right if he sent my first payment in advance, and could I send him twenty-four articles this year? "Yes, yes, and yes," I answered, quickly realizing this meant an extra four hundred dollars per month. Just before hanging up, Chris added, "Oh, and you may have to do a little driving around for your interviews, so I am adding sixteen dollars per week to each month's check."

It wasn't until four days later when the check arrived that I bothered to do the math or comprehended that the sixteen dollars per week, for four weeks, brought the total of every monthly check to exactly four hundred sixty-four dollars. I grabbed my daughters and danced about the kitchen. *Why do I doubt?* I wondered. God, who loves me so, has always been there.

My children, quick to join any celebration, danced and hugged me back, glad to see their mother smiling again.

"Look," I said, holding up the check for their inspection.

"God knew exactly how much money we needed to pay our bills. Aren't we blessed?"

"But didn't you get an E-mail about this, Mom?" Amanda asked.

I had no idea what my child could be talking about. She led me to the computer—and there it was. Two full weeks of almost daily communications with my new editor. I had studied their content carefully and responded promptly, trying to do my best job. I had missed one obvious fact.

"See, Mommy," Amanda said, pointing to my computer mailbox.

My new editor had casually mentioned to me that he pronounced his name "Chris" but spelled it in the traditional Greek way, with a silent "T" on the end. How typical that I had been too absorbed in worries to notice ten transmissions headings clearly marked, "To Linda, from Christ."

Prayers are answered, not in our time, but in His. And always at the right time. Our charge is to live in faith. Not to beg, but to believe.

Christmas Bear

by Timothy Michael Ricke, Casselberry, Florida

It was a cold winter day as eight-year-old Mike ran home from school filled with great excitement. In just two weeks, the annual holiday festival at his school, St. Alexis, would begin. He ran in the front door with a swirl of leaves flying behind him.

"Mom, Mom, can we go to the holiday festival? I want to win the big Christmas bear for Dawn; she'd really like it, don't you think?" He was so excited. His mother smiled and nodded her head in agreement.

Dawn, Mike's little sister, had been bedridden for months with rheumatic fever. Somehow she wore a smile whenever Mike entered the room. She was always so pleased to hear his happy voice. Every day he told her that she was going to get better. Knowing what the odds might be of winning the treasured bear, his mom said, "We can all go to the festival, but let's not discuss the bear with Dawn. We'll make it a surprise, okay?" Mike agreed.

The holiday festival coincided with the first snowfall of the season, adding to the beauty and excitement of the evening for the children. The school band filled the night air with Christmas music. Mike was caught up in the wonder of it all. When he arrived at the school gym, he couldn't wait to "go fish" for the Christmas bear.

He reached deep into his jeans and pulled out the dollar he had earned over the last four months. He gave it to Sister Marie in exchange for a ticket and a plastic fishing pole and seventy-five cents back. Running over to the game, he swung the pole over the curtain. He quickly reeled in a plastic circle with a number on it.

He was puzzled when Sister Martha said, "Michael, go over to that table and give them the circle, and they will give you your prize." She pointed across the room. He quickly ran over to trade his circle for what he thought would be the Christmas bear. His smile vanished as they handed him a noisemaker.

Quickly he exchanged another quarter and went over to the curtain again. He repeated the process until he was out of tickets. Thoroughly disillusioned, he quietly handed back his pole and walked over to his coat, slipped it on, and went outside to sit on the swing by himself. He swung back and forth, drawing lines in the snow with his boots.

That's where his mother found him. "Michael, sometimes things don't always work out for us, and we are disappointed," she gently told him.

He looked up into her eyes and said, "I know, Mom, but I really wanted Dawn to have that bear for Christmas."

"Well, sweetheart," she suggested, "maybe if you pray and believe, perhaps God will help you find a way to have something for your sister this Christmas." Then she repeated her renowned quotation. "Remember, when God closes one door, He leaves another open." Mike shook off the sadness and smiled up at her.

At church that Sunday Mike quietly prayed, "God, would You show me a way to get a present for my little sister? She's been awful sick, and it would really make her feel better." He left church with great faith, believing his prayer would be answered.

On Monday morning, Father Cowth visited each class as usual but ended his morning message with a surprise. "Children, we are going to have a raffle. The money raised will be used to help the poor in our congregation have a joyful Christmas. Children, each ticket sold will be an entry for the contest. The grand prize will be the one item that was not won at the festival, the Christmas bear. The drawing will be on the last day of school before the Christmas break, December 20. But remember, the winner must be present to win." Mike could hardly contain his joy.

Mike made a dash for home. "Mom! Mom! No one won the Christmas bear, and we're going to have a new contest for it!" he shouted with bliss as he burst through the kitchen door. He then proceeded to tell her about the contest and how the bear could be won.

"Well, Michael, looks like you'd better get busy!" she said with assurance in her voice. Away he flew. He canvassed the neighborhood as much as he could and then went downtown to the stores on Main Street. He put his heart and soul into it.

December arrived and Mike had sold only 4 tickets. His friend Ralph had sold 104 tickets through his father's hardware store, which didn't seem fair to Mike, but he did not give up hope. He just prayed over and over again, "Please let me win the Christmas bear for my sister."

He went to bed early the night before the drawing, totally prayed out.

Finally, after hours of prayers and waiting, the moment had arrived. The children assembled in the gym and waited as Father Cowth shook up the box of entries. He reached slowly into the box with eyes closed and pulled out the cherished ticket. He smiled as he looked at the entry. "Okay, children, the winning name is Ralph McGuire. Ralph, come up and get your bear!" Father was delighted because Ralph's family had been very generous to the church, and it only seemed fair.

Mike was close to tears with disappointment and hurt. *I worked so hard and prayed and prayed,* he said to himself.

Once again Father Cowth's voice announced Ralph's name. "Where is Ralph McGuire?" he asked, looking over toward the sisters. Sister Maria told him that Ralph was ill that day. She also reminded Father that the rules required the winner to be present.

"Yes, that's correct, Sister, thank you." So he reached into the box to draw another ticket.

At this point, Mike was so busy feeling sorry for himself that he wasn't paying any attention to what was going on anymore. It confused him when he felt hands patting him on the back and his classmates cheering over and over. "Way to go, Mike!" "Go get it, Mike!"

He'd won! He ran to the front with tears of joy filling his eyes, thinking to himself, *Wow, prayers do work!*

Christmas 1949 was a memorable one. Dawn received her Christmas bear, much to Mike's joy. She also regained her health.

Mike grew up with great faith and hope. To this day, he credits that event with his positive attitude. He's never stopped praying.

Lessons from the Floor

by Lisa Copen, Poway, California

I went to bed about 2:00 a.m. and arose at 7:30, literally creeping to the shower. I was stiff and sore. I had lived for years with rheumatoid arthritis, and after nearly nine months without rain in San Diego, it was pouring that morning. My joints were not pleased with the prospect of awakening.

My husband was still asleep but would be getting up soon. He was taking the day off work to accompany me to a church where I would speak to several chronically ill people about perseverance, faith, taking one day at a time, and relying on God in the midst of life's confusions. I was looking forward to it, as I always gain strength by being around people with illness who depend fully on God.

I felt unprepared, however, as circumstances had given me little opportunity to focus on or prepare for the presentation. As I showered I prayed that God would use me despite my weaknesses. I was far from perfect, but I was doing the best I could. I stepped out of the shower and felt my foot begin to slide. In a flash I realized that I was going down.

In the nine years that I've lived with arthritis, I can count the number of times I have sat on the floor. Once, I was so angry about this illness that was preventing me from doing something that I rebelled by plopping down on the floor, knowing that I would be stuck there until my husband came home. Another time I became irritated by the flashing VCR clock that taunted me; while trying to kneel, I lost my balance.

When I was younger and life's circumstances became overwhelming, I got down on my knees to pray. As a teenager when I felt lost and confused, falling to my knees in prayer brought reassurance. As a college student, dropping to my knees brought comfort that, despite the roommate who wore wanton underwear I didn't even know existed, God was my roommate, too. I expected to wear out lots of kneepads as an adult, but then a chronic illness arrived. Being on my knees now only brought pain and frustration. It reminded me of a past life that I could no longer reach, despite the floor being just inches away.

I went against the instinct to try to catch myself and instead surrendered to the inevitable. I tucked, as the doctor had instructed. "Scratches on the face can heal; broken wrists are not a good thing." I tried to fall toward the carpet but landed on the hard bathroom floor on my left hip and wrist. The stab of pain was great, but even greater was the instant fear that overcame me during the descent. I feared that I would not be able to fulfill my obligations that evening. I could just hear the church announcing, "Our speaker on chronic illness isn't feeling well." That wasn't exactly the kind of credibility that I desired.

After the initial stun of the fall, I slowly gathered my

sprawled limbs and curled them close. I sat. I cried. "Why today, Lord?" I asked. "Why today?" I demanded. My wrist was not broken, but it was useless for a few days. Did God not realize that I already felt less than confident? Satan had already been tantalizing me, making me feel doubtful about my presentation. *Who do you think you are, giving those people advice? You don't know anything more than they do! You still get discouraged, and you still wonder why you have to deal with all of this.* I didn't need physical bruises and a broken spirit this morning.

Finally, I prayed through my tears. The words were the same. "Why, Lord? Why?" But they were filled with a desperate desire to understand, not a demand for an explanation. Then I realized God was determined to remind me that He could always get me on my knees. "Humble yourselves, therefore, under God's mighty hand, that he may lift you up in due time" (1 Peter 5:6).

I was not being humble. My mother would say that God knew I was getting too big for my britches. Despite fears that my message would be less than perfect, I was certain that it wouldn't be difficult. I was a practiced speaker and felt confident in my abilities. I had prayed that God would use my weakness, but was I going to give Him the full credit? My professional self would likely be tempted to credit my abilities to a recent seminar I had attended. Did I want to do well for myself or to really give those people hope? Sure, I am very vocal about giving God the glory, but inside I still feel more pride than I believe would please the Lord.

I had an attitude. I had, I thought, a good excuse for not getting down on my knees. God showed me just how fragile I am without Him. That morning I was too distracted to get the message via a scripture or a praise song. God needed a stronger delivery method to get my attention. I gradually scooted toward a nearby chair. Was it possible to get up? When I was halfway there, my husband heard me yell and came running.

I hadn't lifted myself up. God had lifted me up, physically and spiritually. It hurt, but I got the message. I understood. I made it to the church, and when they looked at me with their tear-filled eyes, broken spirits, and scarred hearts, I told them I am on the same journey as they are. I may have looked like I had it all together, but the mascara, pantyhose, and book table did not represent where I was a few hours ago.

Understanding smiles appeared. Skeptical eyes softened with relief that their struggles were normal. "I sat on the floor and cried huge tears just hours ago because of my illness and how it keeps getting in the way of things," I shared with them. "I felt frustrated and mad and annoyed. I felt like a child who couldn't even get out of the shower properly. I was disheartened because on the one day I needed strength, comfort, and confidence, they were taken from me in an instant. You will fall. We will all have days that we fall in one way or another. But God will pull us all back up. And He knows precisely the unique way to help you up in your circumstances."

Many approached me afterward and said this story made the

difference in how their hearts were touched that evening. I am weak, but He is strong.

God has a plan for our lives, and when we head down the wrong path or get in God's way, He's not timid about pulling the floor out from under us. Just when we think we have a good excuse not to get down on our knees, He reminds us we can always get down on our knees, because without humbling ourselves, there is no need for Him to be there to lift us up.

The Universal Language
by Tony Gilbert, Albany, Georgia

I was in heaven when Georgia hosted the Summer Olympics in 1996. Ever since I was thirteen years old, I had been an Olympic fanatic. My athletic ability (or inability) would never give me the chance to compete, but I was selected as an official for the track and field venue.

Although I could see the Games from the inside, I wasn't about to miss the revelry available to spectators—even if it just meant standing on a street corner watching the crowds. The whole city offered diversions, but entertainment in Centennial Olympic Park was a cultural extravaganza. Thousands of guests from other countries gathered in the name of peace, harmony, and fun. Centennial Olympic Park was a people-watcher's paradise.

Despite spending most of my time in the park that week, my early-bird habits brought me back to my Emory University dorm at a decent hour each evening. That would change on Friday, the first night of track and field competition.

That night, I was officiating the opening round of the men's triple jump. Our event ended about the time I would normally be leaving Centennial Olympic Park. I planned to take a bus back to the dorm, drive into the city, and enjoy the park into the early hours, since I had no duties the next morning.

Boarding the bus behind the stadium, I took off my blazer and pulled down a window. Other officials came aboard, and the bus filled with passengers. Suddenly "The Star-Spangled Banner" filtered from the stadium and into the open bus windows. Everyone reverently listened as it echoed throughout the evening air. We all knew what it meant. An American had won gold in the shot put, the first event to award medals. No one spoke again as the bus pulled away moments later. Everyone was overcome with emotion, pride, and patriotism.

On the way to the dorm, my plans changed. Nothing in Centennial Park could top that. I wanted the highlight of our national anthem echoing through the night air to be my final memory of that night, so I went straight to bed.

That night a bomb exploded in the park just when I'd planned to be there. Two people were dead and dozens injured. I was immediately awake. If I hadn't heard the national anthem echoing inside the bus, I would have been in the park when the bomb exploded.

The next morning I watched SWAT teams investigate the desolate park, which would otherwise be teeming with thousands of visitors. The Olympics took on a more somber mood for three days as the park was closed. The park had been the symbol of these Games, a place for people of the world to gather.

When the gates reopened Tuesday morning, I waited among

the thousands. The masses outside the park were more diverse than before. As I glanced around the crowd, I thought of the words to that simple song, "Red and yellow, black and white, they are precious in His sight. Jesus loves the little children of the world."

We are all His children, I realized, and here we were, with our different colors, costumes, and languages, to renew a spirit that had been lost a few days earlier. A group of Asian students began to sing softly. I knew the tune and joined in my own language, as did most others.

United by the universal language of music and love, we entered the gates while in various tongues we sang, "Mine eyes have seen the glory of the coming of the Lord. . . ."

A Knock at Heart's Door

by Candice Lee Wilber, Denver, Colorado

As a teenager, my life seemed to me a living hell. I had an abusive stepfather whose rage, when I became old enough to try to ignore it, would lead to verbal, and sometimes physical, battles of will. My real daddy, whom I saw very little of, had disappeared out of my life, leaving a false address and broken hearts in his wake. Nothing I did seemed to be worth the effort.

Thinking the solution to our problems was only a "sniff" away, my friends and I finished a bottle of 150-proof Everclear, numbing the present pain but replacing it with an emptiness far more agonizing. The day after that event, feeling so hungover and so sorry for myself that I could find no reason to stay alive, I took a bottle of morphine, hoping to sleep forever. I woke up later, realizing I had failed again.

"God, I hate You!" I raged. I stormed over to my shelves and threw one book after another at my wall, cursing as I went along. I lifted out an old Bible and heaved it the hardest, taking out my bitterness against God and the life He had given me. As I stopped to catch my breath, out of the corner of my eye, I noticed that a page had fallen from the Bible during the crash. Time seemed to stop as I walked across the room, bent over, and picked up the torn page. I stared at it for a long time. The margins were filled with notes in an elegant hand, Jeannie's hand.

My thoughts flew back to a time over a year before; I had been sitting in my bedroom listening to the raucous beat of Metallica when someone knocked on my door. The knock was unlike my stepfather's raging bangs, unlike my mother's "Candice?" punctuated with tentative taps. My brother never knocked at all.

It was a frail, gentle knock, but insistent, as if knocking at my heart's door, afraid of damaging its contents. I carelessly flipped off the stereo, opened the door, and found Jeannie, a widow who attended a Bible study group with my mother, standing in my doorway. I raised an eyebrow at her. Few sane people dared to enter this teenager's room, but she brushed aside magazines, clothing, and candy wrappers; sat down on the floor; and motioned for me to sit beside her.

"I want to give this to you," she said quietly, handing me an expensive-looking, leather-bound book. She started to speak again but seemed to think better of it. Smiling at me, she picked up her long skirt and left, closing the door behind her.

Shrugging, I started to place the book on my shelf, but curiosity proved even stronger than teenage apathy. I carefully opened the thick book to the first page and found the title: *The Holy Bible.* New International Version. I laughed aloud and wondered what right that silly old lady had to give me a Bible! I closed it quickly, as if the pages had burnt my fingers, and placed it on my shelf next to the other dust-covered classics that would be forgotten.

For the first time since that day, I realized the worth of this book to its former owner. With tears streaming down my face, I searched for tape to repair the page and thought about Jeannie: her kindness to strangers and animals; her quiet, gentle voice; her long, elegant hands that had knocked so gracefully on my door a year earlier.

What could have motivated her to give this treasure to an ungrateful teenager who had never taken the time to thank her, much less appreciate the gift? For the first time since the day I had received it, I opened Jeannie's Bible. I think I was looking for the Shepherd Psalm. What I found was Psalm 27:10, "Though my father and mother forsake me, the Lord will receive me."

I never found the Shepherd Psalm that day; sleep overtook me too quickly. But that day proved to be the U-turn that changed my life forever! Two weeks later, at the altar of Christ Episcopal Church, I found a God who understood this frightened, misunderstood child and who loved me unconditionally.

When I went home that evening, I never went to sleep. I read Jeannie's Bible into the early hours of the morning. Within its pages, I found the comfort and answers I had searched for in vain all of my life. It beckoned me to come to a heavenly Father who would never leave, no matter what I had done. I wept as I read the story of the prodigal son, who spent his father's inheritance but was nevertheless welcomed back home with open arms.

The transformation in my life was incredible. The drinking, swearing, and fistfights stopped, and enough outward changes took place to drop the jaws of my classmates the next school year. However, the inward qualities I learned, from daily quiet times reading scripture and spending time with its author, were far more remarkable. Characteristics I had never experienced before emerged: Love replaced hatred; joy replaced depression; hope replaced despair. Becoming a Christian did not solve all my hurts, but God's "peace that passes all understanding" was there like a gentle friend, like the love letter He had authored and sent to me through a weathered but faithful, gentle servant.

Laughing with God on a Bad Hair Day

by Esther Bailey, Phoenix, Arizona

When I started chemotherapy, I thought I was prepared for my loss of hair. I had even quipped to my husband, "Maybe I'll get rid of my dry scalp when my hair comes out."

"It's hardly worth it," Ray replied with a deadpan expression.

From the beginning, I had accepted the news of breast cancer without trauma. Two factors contributed to the sense of peace I experienced throughout each phase of the diagnosis and treatment. A few months earlier, I had been greatly impressed by Dr. Norman Vincent Peale's booklet *Healing for Loved Ones and for You*. The first thing I did when I learned I might have a problem was to reread the faith-building treatise. Any time my faith started to falter, I went back for a refresher course.

Another reason for my upbeat attitude had to do with a statement by my pastor. "Faith that hasn't been tested isn't really faith at all," he said. My life had been quite carefree up to that point. Perhaps it was time for me to learn to deal with adversity.

My surgery went extremely well. They operated on Wednesday, I went home on Thursday, and I attended church on Sunday. I felt surprisingly great!

I elected not to undergo reconstructive surgery because the loss of a breast did not bother me. I simply coined a new slogan: "If you've got it, flaunt it; if you don't, fake it." I was doing okay.

Before starting chemotherapy, I claimed God's promise in Jeremiah 29:11: "For surely I know the plans I have for you, says the Lord, plans for your welfare and not for harm, to give you a future with hope" (NRSV). The verse told me that God would maximize the benefits of chemotherapy and minimize the harmful side effects.

With all that I had going for me, I thought I shouldn't have a problem at all with hair loss. After all, if I could handle losing a breast that wouldn't grow back, surely I could deal with a temporary loss of hair.

"Your hair will probably come out two weeks to the day from the first infusion," the nurse had told me.

When I woke up on the morning of the appointed day, my hair was intact. *Will it survive a wash?* I wondered. As I worked up a lather with the shampoo, my hair began to separate from my scalp. To avoid possibly shedding hair all over the house, I pulled it out by the handfuls. In moments it was gone, and I felt no particular emotion.

Then I looked in the mirror. I was a sorry sight. Looking more like a Martian than an earthling, I quickly donned a turban I had purchased for the occasion. My emotions took a downturn as the day progressed, a situation for which I was not prepared.

That evening, I lamented the loss of my hair to my husband. For the first time in my battle with cancer, tears began to flow.

To me, the turban didn't look much better than my bald head.

"I think you look cute in it," Ray said. When that didn't console me, he added, "I remember seeing Norma Shearer one time in a movie where she wore a turban. She looked pretty and so do you."

Although I appreciated my husband's gallant effort, I still couldn't see it that way. I carried my pity party to bed and didn't sleep well.

My sadness continued the following day. While I was thumbing through a magazine in the afternoon, an article caught my attention. In dealing with the aging process, the author had looked in the mirror and said, "What's so funny, Lord?"

The scene I pictured in my mind put a different spin on my situation. If God was laughing, why not laugh with Him?

As I looked in the mirror with a smile and sparkling eyes, my self-esteem escalated. I took off the turban and discovered that even Martians look better with a happy face.

Before I started chemotherapy, I had my hair cut short, and I started wearing a wig when I went out in public so people wouldn't notice a drastic change. The wig I purchased at a local salon pretty well matched my hair color and style. I didn't want to wear it all the time, though, because it was uncomfortable and hard to keep up.

Even with a positive attitude, I didn't enjoy wearing a turban or a scarf around the house. When I found a catalog showing lightweight wigs at a nominal cost, I decided to experiment. Measuring instructions indicated I needed a petite size, which turned out to be more comfortable. I ordered a short style in a blond color about three shades lighter than my normal hair.

When I tried on the new wig and styled it, I felt like Cinderella—ready for the ball. "I know blonds have more fun," I told Ray, "because I've been blond for only an hour, and I'm having more fun already."

The next day, I wore my new wig to the hospital for a shot. Looking at me with a question mark, the nurse said, "Bailey?"

"Do you notice anything different?" I asked.

"Yes. The wig. I like it."

The improvement of the new wig over the old one was so remarkable that I ordered two more and scrapped the dowdy-looking one.

Compliments poured in from friends at church. I even received a telephone call from someone who had not been able to speak to me in person. My own hair had never caused that much of a sensation.

A couple of weeks later, an elderly man said to me, "I know you've had lots of comments on your hair, but I want to make one more. It's beautiful!"

I smiled and said, "Thank you." I'm sure God was smiling, too.

So what will happen when my hair grows back in? I don't know. Maybe I'll color it and try to match the style of my wig.

After all, if God can laugh at a bad hair day, who am I not to join in?

Project Founder

About the God Allows U-Turns Project Founder

Allison Gappa Bottke lives in southern Minnesota on a twenty-five-acre hobby farm with her entrepreneur husband, Kevin. She is a relatively "new" Christian, coming to the fold in 1989 as a result of a dramatic life "U-turn." The driving force behind the God Allows U-Turns Project, she has a growing passion to share with others the healing and hope offered by the Lord Jesus Christ. Allison has a wonderful ability to inspire and encourage audiences with her down-to-earth speaking style as she relates her personal testimony of how God orchestrated a dramatic U-turn in her life. Lovingly dubbed "The U-Turns Poster Girl," you can find out more about Allison by visiting www.godallowsuturns.com.

About the Contributors

Esther Bailey lives in Phoenix, Arizona, with her husband, Ray. She is a freelance writer with more than eight hundred published credits and is coauthor of two books.

Stephanie Welcher Buckley of Edmond, Oklahoma, is an inspirational writer and speaker. She hosts *State of Change*, a Christian program on KTOK, the highest-rated talk radio station in Oklahoma City. Weekly *State of Change* newspaper columns are syndicated throughout Oklahoma.

Renie Szilak Burghardt is Hungarian by birth and American by choice. A freelance writer with credits in many books and magazines, she lives in Ozark country and loves nature.

Lisa Copen is the founder of Rest Ministries, a nonprofit organization that serves people who live with chronic illness or pain. She is the author of several books and Bible studies for people who are chronically ill, a CLASS graduate speaker, and a freelance writer. She lives in San Diego with her husband, Joel.

Barbara Curtis is an award-winning freelancer with two published books as well as five hundred–plus published articles. Mother to twelve—including three adopted sons with Down's syndrome—Barbara holds a B.A. in Philosophy as well as an AMI Montessori teaching credential.

Wendy Dunham is a wife, a mom, a registered therapist, and a writer whose goal is to do all for the glory of God.

Gerald Eisman of Sarasota, Florida, is a member of the health-care field. A student of human nature, his stories reflect people at their best.

Lowell "Duke" Embs lives in San Antonio, Texas. Before becoming a navy fighter pilot, he graduated from the University of Illinois in 1950. Following his release from active duty, he entered the life insurance business, where he stayed for twenty-six years. During that time, he gathered material for his first book, published in 1995.

Eva Marie Everson is the author of several books and novels. She is a wife, mother, and grandmother and makes her home in Florida.

Tony Gilbert is a writer and consultant living in Albany, Georgia. An accomplished marathon runner, he is also a former teacher, coach, and sports writer.

Patty Smith Hall is an active member of the American Christian Romance Writers. She resides in Hiram, Georgia, with her husband, Dan, and their two daughters, Jennifer and Carly.

Sara Jordan lives in Limestone, Maine. She has been a magazine writer and editor, as well as a writer of short stories for several anthologies.

Carmen Leal is an author and the head of an Internet research site for writers and speakers. She is also coauthor of *Pinches of Salt, Prisms of Light*. In addition to her writing, Carmen is a professional speaker and singer.

Mary J. Dixon Lebeau is an employment counselor, freelance writer, and newspaper columnist. She lives in West Deptford, New Jersey, with her husband, Scott, and her four children.

Iris E. May is published in *GreenPrints* magazine and Liz Curtis Higgs's book *Help, I'm Laughing and I Can't Get Up*. She received an award from the army during Desert Storm for New Wives Training. Married thirty-six years, she is a mother, grandmother, and retired oncology nurse.

Cheryl Norwood lives in Canton, Georgia, just north of Atlanta, with her husband, Mike, in a small World War II bungalow. She has been published in several other anthologies.

Cheryl A. Paden of Fremont, Nebraska, is married and has three sons. She worked for twenty-three years as an RN, retiring to become a freelance writer and lay speaker in the United Methodist Church.

Linda Parker is the author of *The Sand of the Kalahari*, a book on the Bushmen of the Kalahari Desert. Linda is also the mother of two beautiful daughters.

Timothy Michael Ricke is a photographer, writer, Entrepreneur of the Year, and business coach. He resides in Orlando, Florida.

Carol Russell is a writer and speaker. She has had several articles and devotions published, as well as many children's stories. Carol speaks at women's retreats, fellowship meetings, and mother/daughter banquets.

Sandy Sheppard is a pastor's wife, mother of three, freelance writer, and substitute teacher. She is the author of one children's book and over one hundred articles.

Laura Smith resides in Roswell, Georgia, but grew up in Columbus, Ohio. After leasing corporate real estate for ten years, she retired from corporate America to be a stay-at-home mom and to pursue her passion for writing.

Jennifer Smith-Morris loves to help women realize the forgiveness and love they have in Christ Jesus, and she writes and speaks on this topic. She is currently writing a Bible study that teaches and encourages mothers. She lives in Georgia with her husband and three children.

Lynn Roaten Terrell has been published and broadcast around the world. She owns a public relations agency and TheWebDirectory.com Network, which she runs from her historic home in Kansas. Her writing portfolio of award-winning pieces is at LynnTerrell.com. She and Amos, an aerospace engineer, have two children.

Jo Upton is a freelance writer with more than fifteen years of experience. Her work has appeared in magazines, books, newsletters, and various Web sites. She is married with four children and two grandchildren.

Candice Lee Wilber lives in Longmont, Colorado. She is a full-time music teacher and young-adult novelist. She lives with her husband, Patrick, and their pet hermit crabs.

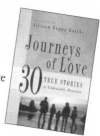

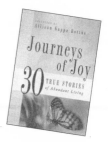